Interiors book of

HOTELS & MOTOR HOTELS

Interiors book of

HOTELS & MOTOR HOTELS

by Henry End, A.I.D., I.D.I.
With an Introduction by
Lawson A. Odde

Whitney Library of Design, New York

Design: Gary Fujiwara

Typesetting: Letterpress — Miller-Johnson, Inc.

Offset — NuType Service

Printing: Letterpress — Miller-Johnson, Inc.

Offset — Robert Teller Sons & Dorner

Binding: Russell-Rutter Co., Inc.

Library of Congress Catalog Card No. 62-18474

© 1963

Whitney Library of Design,

Charles E. Whitney, President;

William Wilson Atkin, Vice-President.

A Division of Whitney Publications, Inc.

18 East 50th Street, New York 22, N. Y.

Publishers of Interiors and Industrial Design

TABLE OF CONTENTS

To Jessica
My Undesigning Wife

INTRODUCTION

Let us begin this introduction by saying that the American Hotel & Motel Association is strongly in favor of professionalism in the food and lodging industry. We believe that there is no substitute for knowledge and experience and, hence, are constantly working to improve both as they affect our members and the industry as a whole.

This is, perhaps, why Henry End's book intrigues us so much. For in it he compounds a strong argument for professionalism in design, an argument to which the members of our industry had best pay heed since so great a part of an establishment's chances for success rest with tasteful design.

One of the great problems facing the innkeeping industry today is overbuilding. The American Hotel and Motel Association does not object to new construction per se but it does find fault with unwarranted expansion where economic realities make financial loss a certainty on both the new property and the existing ones. In many areas of our nation there are at present many more lodging accommodations available than there are people to use them and occupancy rates tumble on a yearly basis.

Yet some establishments are immediate or continuing successes. Who are the successful innkeepers of today? They are, in the vast majority of cases, persons whose background and training have prepared them for administrative positions in our industry — and this holds true whether an individual is the head of a giant corporation or the sole owner of a 10-unit motel.

It is every bit as fallacious for an individual to risk his and his wife's life savings on a small motel as it is for a corporation to pour a few million dollars into a new operation if this money, in either case, is going to go down the drain. We, at the American Hotel & Motel Association, have always urged that persons thinking of building a new lodging property engage the services of a survey firm to predict the feasibility of the investment.

These studies should include location, competition, expected volume of business, and many other facts. Only after carefully weighing all the pros and cons of this report should anyone venture a capital investment for a new set of accommodations.

It would seem to us, therefore, that if overbuilding is a problem, lack of professionalism is perhaps one of its biggest causes. There seems to be something about the innkeeping business that attracts people and money and disillusionment is apt to be rapid.

The mistakes made by amateurs in this regard are legion, the mistakes made by professionals are rare. And thus we return to Henry End's proposition that the thinking innkeeper will use professionals — in architecture, in landscaping, and in interior design.

There is something about newness that attracts guests. This is an undeniable fact. But newness is not enough to hold a guest or encourage him to return time after time. The extras — the plus marks — in a guest's stay are often those items which command little attention: personal service, pleasant attitudes, living up to certain standards. And let's not forget design.

Mr. End points out, quite candidly, that too often owners intrude their way into a designer's work. In most cases where this has occurred, the results have been disastrous for the owner is almost never a professional designer. In addition the designer should be called in at the start of a project rather than after it is under way and the architect has had a chance to indelibly stamp his trademark on those things which are properly the area of the interior designer.

How much better to have tasteful decor than an initially spectacular one which quickly bores and then sours the guest on returning? Mr. End tells us that this is the case in many properties. The result is costly redecoration or a loss in business which often means loss of investment. Much more desirable is the use of a designer from the inception through completion of a new project.

In the innkeeping industry employees must be better trained and more skilled than ever. The American Hotel & Motel Association works in this area, through its Education Institute — to train employees, to increase the value of service to guests, and to raise the profits of individual establishments. As this program spreads, so will the level of excellence among employees.

Let us sum up this introduction of a fine book by saying that Henry End expounds those ideas upon which we place great value — that professionalism in our industry is the most important factor which can lead to success, that it is the base upon which the profitable aspects of innkeeping depend.

Not every innkeeper is successful, but every successful innkeeper is a professional.

Lawson A. Odde
EXECUTIVE VICE-PRESIDENT
AMERICAN HOTEL AND MOTEL ASSOCIATION

Interiors book of

HOTELS & MOTOR HOTELS

Palace Hotel, San Francisco, Calif., The Bettmann Archive

Tremont House

I—THE HERITAGE

It was appropriate that the cornerstone of the first grand hotel was laid on a July Fourth.

The year was 1828 and the place was Boston. The hotel was the Tremont, a truly American invention designed to satisfy the craving of a young nation for status. For anyone able to pay $2.00 a day it opened a realm of elegance, grandeur, and ostentation that had always been reserved for the nobility and landed gentry of the old world.

Nothing like the Tremont had ever been seen. There were 170 rooms and all of them were carpeted. It had the first lobby that was not a bar room. The floor was marble and the decorating was in the French style. It was the first hotel to have a clerk greeting the guests; the first to have a bowl and pitcher in the room and even a bar of free soap; the first to have French cuisine; the first to have room keys. These were attached to a small piece of iron so the guests would not carry them off by mistake. Hotels gradually gave up on such precaution, but the forgetfulness of the customers increased at such a rate that Congress in 1926 passed a special bill making it possible to return hotel keys by collect mail.

The bar at the Tremont was like the drawing rooms of the grandest of palaces. In his *American Notes,* Charles Dickens wrote that in this bar, "The stranger is initiated into the mysteries of gin sling, sherry cobbler, mint julep, songaree, timber doodle and other rare drinks." A young architect named Isaiah Rogers designed the Tremont in the classic Greek style that was to dominate fashion for more than half a century. The most astounding thing about the hotel was the lack of a carriage entrance. Here it broke completely with a tradition that had ruled innkeeping for hundreds of years.

THE ENGLISH INN

In 1551, there is a reference in English law to the inn. It appeared in an act ordering magistrates to secure bonds from innkeepers to assure order. It was the same type of restraint as was placed on owners of ale houses. In 1603-04, a legal distinction was made between the two . . . "since the ancient and principal true use of Innes and Victuallinge Houses was for the Receipte, Relief and Lodginge of wayfaring people travellinge from place to place." The innkeeper was given duties and privileges beyond that of the alehouse owner, but the license to operate a hotel in England today is still basically one of an excise nature; that is, to sell wines and spirits.

The stagecoach and the inn developed together for the 200 years before the railroad appeared in the 1840s. Many innkeepers established their own coach systems to bring in customers for bed and board. The Royal Inn at Cheltenham (England) offered a score of coach services, including waiting rooms and reservations. Gradually, the larger inns added assembly rooms designed to meet the social needs of the town or village, just as the modern hotel has come to depend on the luncheon and dinner trade of the Kiwanis and Rotary clubs. At the George Inn at Stamford, there is a survival of the stagecoach era above the doors of the north and south dining rooms. They are labeled "Edinburgh" and "London." It is interesting that the Tabord Inn of Chaucer's "Canterbury Tales" could boast of everything that a modern hotel needs to operate. It had a sign, a host, a staff of servants, table d'hote meals, and a bill.

By 1550, an architectural style had been developed for the English Inn and it held to form until the railroad appeared. The entrance from the street was through an arched carriageway to a cobblestone courtyard. The kitchen and the public rooms faced the street. The guestrooms were along the galleries overlooking the courtyard. In the rear were stables for horses.

(To skip forward several centuries for a moment, an old Wisconsin statute still on the books in 1961, required that an innkeeper provide lodging for a guest's horse at not more than fifty cents a night. And the Milwaukee Inn, a modern motor hotel, found itself forced to care for a horse in the parking lot during a convention of the Wisconsin Quarter Horse Association. This was done simply as a publicity gag, but it does remind us of the tie the 20th century motel has with the hostler of earlier years.)

The word "hotel", considered pretentious by the early innkeepers of England, goes back a long way. In medieval Latin, it was "hospitale." In old French, it was "ostelerie." By 1500 the words "hostler" and "ostler" had come to mean an inn servant. Perhaps that was one of the reasons the English inn never really amounted to much, even in service and cleanliness, although in the 18th century they were accounted amongst the best in the world. In his book, *The American Hotel*, Jefferson Williamson wrote:

> English inns never went beyond a certain point, and the English innkeeper remained a traditionalist, unwilling or unable to get out of his ages-old rut, and content to let well enough alone. Meanwhile, the American landlord showed not the slightest fear of turning all sorts of new corners. He had become an expansionist and an innovator, first surpassing his English contemporary in

2

ASTOR HOUSE

the size of his establishments and eventually eclipsing him in other respects.

As we shall see later, in the chapter on International Hotels, the situation had not changed a century later when American corporations began putting up hotels in areas of traditional British influence and in the heart of London itself.

A former newspaperman, Williamson wrote his anecdotal history of the industry while he was editing the *Hotel Gazette* between 1924 and 1930, the year he died. The book was published posthumously by Alfred A. Knopf and is now out of print, but it remains the one great source of information about the growth of an industry that mirrored the restlessness and vitality of a young nation. Williamson pointed out that it took 12,000 years for innkeepers to progress to the point of having 30 rooms under one roof. And in the next 100 years this jumped to 3,000 rooms.

THE HOTEL IN AMERICA

In America, the hotel became the focal point of social activities for a growing middle class. It is today the place to salute achievement, whether this be the installation of a realty board president or the $1,000-a-plate dinners for charity and politics. It is a residence for those who have achieved greatness; this could be dispossessed royalty or the retired general of the armed forces. And typically American is the fact that the grandeur of hotel

3

Astor House, New York City

life is available to all who have the price, whether it be the bootblack who
strikes it rich in the stock market or the red-necked cattleman come to
town to sell his thousand head of white faced Herefords.

Hotels are closely involved with civic pride. Certainly this is what drove
John Jacob Astor to build Astor House in New York. If Boston could have
its Tremont, New York deserved something bigger and better. Was it
coincidence that Astor used the same architect and also selected July 4th
for his cornerstone ceremony? Probably not. More a case of emphasizing
that "anything you can do, I can do better." Astor House, opened in 1836,
was two floors higher than Tremont, and had 309 rooms. It also had its
own gas plant and a steam engine to help with kitchen chores and pump
water to the upper floors. Greeley's *New Yorker* said in its edition of June
4, 1836, "We believe it does not stipulate any assistance in bed-making,
sweeping rooms, dusting furniture, attending on guests, etc., but in the

Copyright.   STATE STREET, CHICAGO.   By permission Chicago Eng. Co.

onward march of improvement, we may expect all this to follow in good time." Mayor Philip Hone predicted that the Astor would serve as a monument to its wealthy proprietor for centuries to come, but within thirty years Astor House was a second-rate hotel.

And so it went for more than a century. As the railroads spread westward across the continent, new cities grew at junction points. With new cities came new chambers of commerce that realized the need for a grand hotel to demonstrate enterprise and faith in the future. These hotels were not imitations of the ones that went up in New York, Philadelphia, and Boston. They were grander and better.

Obsolescence was no great problem in the last half of the 19th century. Fire usually took care of that. The big one in Chicago in 1871 wiped out practically every big hotel but before the coals were cool four new ones were going up, each of them grander than anything standing in New York. The four included a new Palmer House with its 225 silver dollars in the tiled floor of the barbershop. This was not Potter Palmer's idea. William Eaton figured it was a perfect way to get people in for a haircut and a shave; they had to come down to prove to themselves that some idiot had buried money in the floor. It turned out to be one of the great publicity stunts in the history of the industry and one that was picked up by countless saloons throughout the west.

THE SAN FRANCISCO PALACE

The push continued westward to San Francisco where the grandest of hotels went up in 1875. The Palace cost five million and its 775 rooms made it the biggest city hotel in the world. That same year the United States Hotel opened with 1,000 rooms in Saratoga Springs, but that was a resort.

Like many of the grand hotels of all times, the Palace was a white elephant in its early days; eventually, however, it made money. Seven floors high, it covered an entire block. The crystal-roofed central court was a throw-back to the inn courtyard, but there were no strolling players performing on cobblestones. The Palace court was 144 feet by 48 feet and an orchestra played each afternoon and evening in a tropical garden setting. The Palace was doomed by the 1906 earthquake and fire, but three years later a new one rose from the ashes.

As he neared the completion of his book in 1930, Williamson looked back at a decade that had seen hotels built at such a fantastic rate that 5,000 rooms had been added each year. With that as the background and with the new Waldorf-Astoria and Pierre hotels going up, the editor felt secure in commenting that, "The big basic forms of mechanical service, such as plumbing and heating, elevators, lighting, telephones, ventilation are now all thoroughly developed and perfected and perhaps will no longer have a share in making hotels obsolete — though," he quickly added, "one cannot be certain about that." Much the same caution is necessary nowadays in face of the temptation to think that the hotel of the jet age is just about the ultimate in design, comfort, and ingenuity. It is highly probable that the author of a book on hotels three decades from now will be discussing the problems of rocket blast-offs. And who knows what issues architects and designers will face with the Lunar Hilton and the Venus Sheraton?

The great advantage of a hotel is that it's a refuge from home life.

George Bernard Shaw
"Cashel Byron's Profession"

The Bettmann Archive

United States Hotel, Saratoga Springs, N. Y.

THE AIR AGE

Williamson could count the American hotels clustered about railroad terminals across the nation and it led him to observe, "Locations in most American cities have, by this time, become fairly stabilized, but may have to be readjusted if travel by air supersedes all present modes of travel." Three decades later the airlines of the world were carrying travelers at the rate of nearly a billion passenger miles a year and the projection for 1970 was for more than triple that figure. The airport had become a magnet for the major hotel developers, just as the railroad station had been a century ago.

Like the riddle of the chicken and the egg, it is still debated which comes first: the traveler or the hotel. As America's cities blossomed across the Great Plains and into the West, civic leaders and real-estate speculators both gambled that if the hotel were there the people would come, and that seeing the hotel the stranger would be convinced that here indeed was a dynamic metropolis.

The outburst of nationalism following World War II has produced those same moving forces. The grand hotel is a symbol of national pride and ambition in the most remote of the new republics. Tomorrow they will be less remote and their hotels will show the world that these nations have made the leap into the 20th century.

II—HOTELS IN TOWN

You could have gotten long odds in the early 1950s had you been willing to bet that the downtown hotel would ever stage a comeback in the United States.

The nation was traveling at a record rate, but all the business appeared to be headed for the sparkling motels springing up in the suburbs and along the expanding highway system. The downtown hotel, worn and tired from its wartime service, seemed doomed. The better ones were being seized by Hilton and Sheraton in a chain reaction related to tax laws and the complicated business of depreciation and loss carry-overs.

In Volume LI No. 1, *Fortune* magazine surveyed the industry and concluded, "With new construction costs figured at anywhere from $16,000 to $30,000 a room, the large-scale building of large city hotels doesn't seem to be imminent." Exactly six years later, the magazine took another look and found a "remarkable comeback of the downtown hotel, an institution that a decade ago was considered well on the road to oblivion." The editors spotlighted the great concentration of prime hotel rooms by Hilton and Sheraton, each doing a more than two million dollars a year business. In searching for the answer to the resurgence of the hotel business, *Fortune* looked to the urban renewal programs that made strategic sites available and to the creation of new convention centers around the country. Another factor was the 1954 tax bill provision which allowed fast depreciation and attracted a lot of speculative capital into new hotel ventures.

But there is another answer and it can be found in the last page of Jefferson Williamson's book on the American Hotel. In 1930, the year he died, the editor of the *Hotel Gazette* contemplated two buildings then under construction: the Waldorf-Astoria and the Pierre. Though he was dazzled by their dimensions and grandeur, Williamson concluded:

> Our national appetite for luxury will only be whetted by these
> two examples of what hotels may be, and it is safe to predict
> that very soon Mine Host will be planning others to equal them
> in magnificence. For the history of the hotel in America is the
> history of progressive luxury, and it is not to be assumed that its
> end has been reached.

With occupancy rates continuing to slide and the trade press in 1962 warning against the building of more rooms, one might wonder why anyone would put up a new hotel. Curt Strand, Vice President of Hilton International, has these reasons:

New hotels must be built either because they are needed (even if part of the financing of overseas projects must come from government) or because obsolete hotels must be replaced. They must be built even if the number of vacant rooms would indicate caution. We don't want to become obsolete as a company.

According to William Ebersol, general manager of Hotel Pierre in New York:

With few exceptions, the new hotel is the investor's and community's way of overcoming obsolescence of current accommodations.

The factor of community responsibility and spirit takes on real meaning when you consider the booster spirit of a town like Dallas. Here was a new breed of millionaires determined to demonstrate they could do anything New York, Los Angeles, or Chicago could do, and perhaps do it better.

SHERATON-DALLAS

Sheraton came into Dallas as part of a complex built by Southland Life Insurance Company and designed by Welton Becket Associates of Los Angeles (see illustrations, page 24). It consisted of two cleanly modern towers: a 42-story office building for the insurance company and a 29-story, 600-room hotel turned at right angles to its big brother. Although the center occupies an entire block, Becket separated the two buildings by a three-quarter acre plaza of landscaping and terrazzo paving. He did have to tie the buildings together with a shopping arcade and a glass-enclosed concourse at the second-floor level because under Texas law an insurance company could have ownership in only one building to be used as home offices. The legal aspects of the situation were strengthened when Becket put all the convention facilities of the hotel over on the second floor of the insurance building to keep them away from the slimmer guestroom tower of the hotel. There he had plenty of space for two major meeting areas. Both the grand ballroom and the republic suite on the second floor of the office tower can be divided into separate areas and there is an excellent system of folding partitions to do the work. Also on this floor is the main kitchen with easy access to the convention rooms and to the two restaurants on the concourse.

While the exterior form of the center is typically severe, Becket used prefabricated panels of blue-green and cerulean glass mosaic tile that fit in the curtain wall system. The sheer walls are precast concrete with some aggregates of granite and quartz exposed to give the towers sparkle. For the literal minded, there are 38,500,000 of the tiles in the window-wall panels, each of them five-eighths of an inch square.

This was one of the rare times Becket did not handle the interiors himself, for Sheraton has a strong design staff headed by Mary Morrison Kennedy who was trained as an architect. Her style has invariably leaned to the traditional but in the Sheraton-Dallas there was a recognition that a more contemporary feeling was needed to complement the architecture. In the lobby areas are handsome steel and black leather benches, teak paneling, and square columns of black marble. Art plays a major role in lending warmth and local color to Southland Center. On one wall of the concourse that connects the two towers is a mosaic mural by Gyorgy Kepes and Robert Preusser. The abstract is entitled *Texas Sun*. As the guest stands before the registration desk faced with beige Milano marble, he is treated to the sight of an immense mural executed in Venetian glass and marble by Lumen Martin Winter. Called *Stampede,* its brilliant colors dominate the otherwise subdued tones of the lobby.

To get to the second-floor lobby and convention rooms, the guests have a choice of escalators, elevators, or a spectacular staircase sculptured in concrete and steel. In the well of the staircase, and extending to the ceiling of the lobby is a stabile by Richard Filipowski. The red, sapphire blue and gold sculpture in metal and glass is entitled *Totem*. Except for the fanciful *People in Space* mural done by Estelle and Erwine Laverne for the Orbit cocktail lounge, the artwork is oriented pretty much to the southwest. The murals by Edward Laning for the Republic of Texas suite tell the history of the state with emphasis on the roles played by Sam Houston, Stephen Austin, and William B. Travis.

For the guest who arrives under a ten gallon hat, and most of them do, there is a touch of home underfoot in the lobby. A longhorn design was woven into the gold carpets made in Hong Kong.

Except for the baroque Presidential Suite, which was done presumably to give an impression of costliness, the interiors of the guestrooms reflect the influence of the architectural style of Southland Center. On each floor are nine studio rooms, four twin bedrooms, and two doubles. Mrs. Kennedy devised six decorative schemes so that no adjacent rooms are alike. The rooms are generous in size — a minimum of fourteen feet square. The wall-to-wall carpeting is light in color but with a clever pattern that resists stains.

THE DENVER HILTON

The Sheraton and the hotel that Hilton took over with the acquisition of the Statler chain have given real impetus to the growth of downtown Dallas. The same thing happened in Denver when William Zeckendorf added a 21-story hotel to his Mile High Center. Designed by I. M. Pei and Associates, the 884-room hotel had an early history of trouble until the Hilton organization came into the picture and the ownership was turned over to the Allegheny Corporation to settle some debts.

This is truly a grand hotel with a monumental approach. It has received extravagant praise from design and architectural critics. Wrote John Anderson, then managing editor of *Interiors:*

This is not a home-away-from-home, but a hotel that glamorizes the adventure of holidays, conventions, and even business trips. The lobby floor, extending the length of the tower, is a masterwork of emotional articulation in which all elements build one upon the other to the creation of a single poetic expression.

He also wrote of the

expressiveness of its highly atmospheric interior spaces, the humanizing roles of specially designed furniture and interior appointments, and the focusing lift and charm of specially commis-

The traveling salesman on the road these days never had it so good — and neither, for that matter, did the farmer's daughter on vacation with her husband and five children.

Time Magazine

11

sioned art works — all to the ultimate end of affording humans a certain sense of the marvelous.

I. M. Pei is an exceptionally brilliant architect of the "International" school; his work is clean and slick, but lacking in soul. With the interiors of the Denver Hilton he has taken an approach typical of the international style. There is so little warmth and coziness that one envisions guests wandering through the lobby areas bewildered and a little stunned by the scale and the art work. It could just as easily be an office building on Wall Street or Park Avenue in New York (see illustrations, page 26).

What the architect set out to do, he did well. He used the modularly designed furniture in groupings as if he were handling building blocks; the lounge areas, for instance, would be highly acceptable for a bank. This is not to imply that interior design must mean that every wall and surface be decorated with sconces and plaques — materials like marble and tile can be embellishment enough in themselves. However, the public areas of the Denver Hilton create such a monumental feeling that there is a danger of making the guest feel puny and insignificant. In theory, of course, such use of space might serve to elevate and this could well be true in practice, but it would depend on whether the guest is more extroverted than introverted. It is probably safer to create more warmth and intimacy than to rely on a particular psychological propensity.

What little texture there is in the lobby areas is incorporated in the ingenious ceiling designed by Alexander Girard, although it is debatable that many of the guests are even aware it is up there; and there is a coldness about the Harry Bertoia tree sculptures that grow from the terrazzo floor.

In other words, one gets the impression that in creating these grand spaces, Pei has neglected the human relationship. Take the cocktail lounge as an example. The circular bar with its backless stools gives a feeling of being in a railroad station waiting room. It is interesting that the editors of *Architectural Forum* were enchanted by the original guestroom design by the Pei staff when Zeckendorf still had control of the hotel, but of the subsequent interiors done for Hilton by Elliott Frey and Associates, design division of Duo-Bed Corporation, *Forum* complained about "mail-order-taste furnishings." In the author's opinion, Frey did an excellent job of the guest rooms; his furnishings are comfortable and work well and in each room he incorporated something of the history of Colorado.

THE SUMMIT

At the other end of the spectrum for hotel design is the Summit which was opened by Laurence and Preston Tisch in 1961, the first Manhattan hotel in thirty years (see illustrations, page 32). Fantastically successful in Atlantic City and then in South Florida, the Tisch brothers built the 800-room Summit at a reported cost of eighteen million on scarcely 100 feet of frontage along Lexington Avenue. The architect-designer was Morris Lapidus who had gained world-wide fame for his grandiose hotels in Miami Beach. He had given the Tisch brothers the Americana there, and it ranks as one of the most successful resort hotels in the world.

In the summer of 1961, Larry and Bob Tisch sent out engraved invita-

The technical problems will be fairly standard wherever the hotel is built. But the hotel visitor wants more than efficiency.

Stephen Garrett
Design

tions for the "opening of New York's first new luxury hotel in thirty years." It was a big event, but the reaction was a stunning one for owners and architect alike. *Time Magazine* called it "something between Bronx baroque and Mexicali modrun." Comedians began arguing over who was first to coin the line, "The Summit is all right, but it's too far from the beach." It got so rough that even the Tisches decided something must be wrong and they told Lapidus to tone the place down, to lower the lighting and use some browns and tans instead of a potpourri of brilliant colors.

The Summit is an example of what happens when architects and designers attempt to be overly dramatic. Considering the difficult site and the owners' demand for so many rooms, Lapidus did a remarkable job. But, then, he should have stopped to consider that the Summit was on Lexington Avenue in New York, not on Collins Avenue in Bal Harbour, Florida. A certain amount of liberty can be taken with color and textures in a resort hotel, but to attempt the same gambit in downtown Manhattan was folly. It is a common fault of many hotel designers to try to crowd too much into the job. Public spaces are smaller today. They cannot be stuffed with all the gimmicks that were considered a must for the hotels that went up three decades ago. And it must now be obvious to all that Miami Beach does not belong in New York City.

In defense of the Summit, Lapidus told *Interior Design* magazine that the motivation of all of his work was "satisfying the emotional hunger of man's primitive love of adornment (the basis of all art), refined and developed, millenium after millenium, expressed in the idiom of today, remembering yesterday, groping for tomorrow." He acknowledged that he had been ignored and sometimes condemned by the architectural press for the design and interiors of hotels. But he answered, "These same hotels are quite well known and admired by the general public." To be sure, there are enough visitors to New York who will accept the Summit, people who mistake pretentiousness for glamour. Nevertheless, the hotel will in all probability be dated within a few years; time will teach the lesson that the architect and designer must lead public taste, not cater to its lowest common denominator.

In principle, Lapidus' theory that hotels should be places of excitement is a sound one; the whole question boils down to the matter of degree. The circus is probably man's most exciting invention, but it is a rare person who wants to stay there for more than a couple of hours. Before it was toned down, the lobby of the Summit blazed with light that was bounced from terrazzo floors with inlays of greens and blues, from a registration desk faced with colored mosaics, and from elevator doors in blue, purple, turquoise, and black porcelain enamel.

A basic problem with the Summit stemmed from the public relations campaign that forecast it as a luxurious and elegant addition to the New York scene. In actual fact, it was to be strictly a commercial hotel and all the distraction of color, lighting, and decorative icing in the lobby and restaurants could not disguise the fact. With a ten-acre site in Miami Beach, there is a chance of pulling off an aura of magnificence. On a long, narrow strip of costly Manhattan real estate, it was impossible.

In a penetrating article on the Summit, *Interiors* editor, Olga Gueft,

True comfort requires more than meeting the hotel guest's physical needs. The hotel must also satisfy deep emotional needs as well. A hotel can have an uncomfortable atmosphere even when every physical need is met. Emotional comfort must be achieved and a person away from home, for whatever reason, unconsciously expects a new experience, an emotional lift.

Morris Lapidus, Architect

reviewed the importation of the "sun-dazzled carnival world of Miami Beach" to New York. She made this observation:

> Bowling matches in the lower lobby of the majestic, arc-shaped Fontainebleau could not possibly disturb quiet conversations in the upper; the fact that the Fontainebleau is a resort hotel and the Summit a commercial hotel does not really account for the difference. In the Fontainebleau every space, every piece of furniture seems larger than life. In the Summit, every space is mean.

Miss Gueft blames the Tisch brothers for demanding that Lapidus somehow distract the public from realizing that the Summit was an 800-room commercial hotel jammed into a small space. She also blamed the architect for attempting to pull off the trick. But there is a recognition of the architect's skill in the use of the lighting in the lobby, columns in alternating dark and light tones to de-emphasize their presence, simple fishnet curtains at the lobby windows, and changes from plain to patterned in corridor carpeting to reduce the tunnel effect. At the other extreme, Miss Gueft pointed out, there is the specialty restaurant

> where the cut-up levels and the large murals looming on the rough-textured claustrophobic walls make you see imaginary mirrors where there are none . . . the result of Lapidus' frantic effort to confuse the eye is simply: confusion.

Had all this stopped in the public spaces, the guest might have found the antidote in his bedroom. But even upstairs the effect tended to be restless when tranquility should have been the goal. The hotel lobby must certainly be an area of attraction, a gathering place. It is the showcase of the hotel and here the designer can do things which are monumental, exciting, and glamorous. He has the scale to work with and the appeal can be very broad. On the other hand, the guestroom should provide privacy and intimacy, elements that give the guest a certain feeling of naturalness. A guestroom should not be decorated to generate excitement as it is primarily a place for sleeping, for resting, and for lounging.

THE MATTER OF TASTE

Perhaps the biggest problem in hotel design is to do things in good taste without the elements of either catering to any popular level or attempting to "elevate" the public taste. A conscious effort at either one will put the designer on dangerous ground with the risk of creating vulgarity on the one hand and uneasiness on the other. Too earnest an attempt to elevate the guest will merely make him uncomfortable. For example, using abstract paintings such as might be found in the Guggenheim Museum would in most hotels be dangerous. There are too many people who would not understand the approach and would get the feeling that somebody was making fun of them.

The designer must find that hard-to-find happy medium. He must do things which are high style and different enough to be interesting, without being clichés, gaudy, or mundane. A certain amount of exuberance is acceptable, but it must be cleverly controlled. Once over the bounds of good taste, there is no return.

One of the finest essays on good taste can be found in *Decoration and Furniture*, Volume Two of *Principles of Modern Design* by Bruce Allsopp, ARIBA. This book, by the lecturer in architecture at the University of Durham, England, was published by Sir Isaac Pitman & Sons and is a provocative lesson in design.

Allsopp says good taste is hard to define, but he adds,

It is generally thought to be essential that decoration be in good taste, and one might almost be tempted to say that taste is really a matter of opinion, varies from time to time, and is dependent upon the current opinions of people whose social prestige is high. But there is more in it than that. The standard of good taste was certainly set, to a large extent, by the aristocracy in the 18th century, and it is now set, to as great an extent, by critics whose business it is to assess the value of contemporary work, and to publicize what they regard as good; by designers themselves who have a larger part in forming taste than they ever had; by councils and societies whose members are often critics or designers; by schools of architecture and design; and probably to a less extent by merchants, salesmen, and advertisers. The modern patron also has his say, but he seems to be more passive than his aristocratic predecessor. Time may change this, but it is interesting to note that the man who pays for a design is now called the client. It used to be the artist who was his patron's client. The word has completely changed its meaning since the nineteenth century, in which, for perhaps the first time in history, the architect was able to exploit his patron to the disadvantage of both.

He goes on to warn against those who talk of good taste as if it were something akin to geometry. That is, a science for which there are certain firm principles. He argues that standards of taste

are most easily appreciated, not by any set of positive rules, but by considering what good taste does not permit.

Stop to consider how much fine work has succeeded because of what was left in the warehouse or on the showroom floor!

Allsopp says the greatest danger for the designer lies in pretentiousness.

A certain amount of ostentation, according to the period, may be allowable, but any pretence of wealth and grandeur is in bad taste. The best examples of this kind of bad taste are to be seen in the foyers of many "super" cinemas where seemingly costly effects are obtained by cheap and often tawdry means, such as plastic paint heavily textured and gilded with artificial gold paint, cheap reliefs in plaster emulating real sculpture, but lacking any artistic content, and mural paintings which have been turned out by the square yard and usually anonymously, the ghastly secret of their authorship being locked in the archives of some firm of painters and decorators.

Allsopp also reminds us of the women who can appear chic in a

Fewer and fewer young people seem to have an understanding of taste and that is true of many older people as well, but an overwhelming number think they have, probably because they confuse their personal preferences for taste.

Walter Hoving, Chairman Tiffany and Company

simple cotton dress while others

dress extremely badly at enormous cost, ruining the creations
even of the most artistic coutouriers, whenever they let their own
taste affect their costume in any way. It is the same with decoration and furniture.

And one more brilliant line.

Taste is not enough. There must be vivacity and originality. Paradoxically, the best taste is poised upon the edge of the unknown,
upon the brink of disaster.

PITTSBURGH HILTON

Sometimes, the hotel designer is foiled in his concept by such mechanical objects as air conditioning and sound systems. In the case of the
Pittsburgh Hilton (see illustrations, page 34) there seems to have been
a complete lack of collaboration between the designers and the engineers.
Everywhere one looks there are ventilating ducts and outlets with no relationship to the interior design.

The architectural design by William Tabler of this 24-story building
is far better than the design of the interiors. In the latter there appears
to be too much going on at the same time, a busyness that never settles down.
As in all chain hotels, the Hilton studio has incorporated examples of local
art. Several designers on the faculty of Carnegie Institute contributed art
work in stainless steel, aluminum, and black tile representing Western
Pennsylvania's three major industries. In most of the public spaces there
is the distraction of mechanical systems for which there is really little
excuse. In the Edgewater Beach Hotel in Chicago, for instance, the air
conditioning system for the ballroom was incorporated into the lighting
coves so that it became part of the interior design.

EXECUTIVE HOUSE

The appeal of new sparkling hotel rooms in downtown areas of our
older cities is substantiated by the success of Executive House, which went
up in 1958 near the Loop in Chicago (see illustrations, page 31). The
first major hotel built in Chicago in nearly thirty years, it is one of the
tallest (40 stories) reinforced concrete structures in the country.

Executive House, designed by Milton M. Schwartz and Associates,
was originally planned as an apartment hotel and many of the 448 units
were to be rented to permanent guests; even the one-room studios were
equipped with a small kitchen and bar. However, because of the shortage
of new hotel rooms for transient guests downtown, the hotel found no need
to push the leasing of rooms and suites. There is no doubt the financing
was found more easily for the seven million dollar project because of the
apartment living facilities. Investors still have not forgotten the hundreds
of hotels that were washed into the bankruptcy courts during the depression
of the 1930s.

Because the Loop with its bevy of amusements is so close, there was
no need to build a lot of public space into Executive House. There is almost
no lobby at all and only a restaurant and bar on the ground level while at

*Designing and planning is the most important service offered a contract consumer. Every job must begin with a
plan and since interiors are to be used
by people, the first consideration in the
work is human engineering. Then, aesthetics are introduced to make the space
attractive.*

*J. William Keithan, General Manager
Western Service & Supply Company
From: Hotel Monthly*

roof level there are meeting rooms and a solarium cocktail lounge. The hotel guests can entertain easily in the rooms which have a delightful residential atmosphere enhanced by a large (six feet by nineteen feet) balcony set into the facade of the building. Colors are subdued to give a sense of comfort and the styling of the interiors is in a smart contemporary vein.

DUPONT PLAZA CENTER

An uncommon hotel built in recent years is Dupont Plaza Center (see illustration, page 30) in downtown Miami. The 12-story building combines a hotel with 250 rooms, an office building, and an architect's sample bureau. It was designed as a commercial hotel, but only five miles away is the greatest collection of resort hotels in the world; the goal became the creation of a business hotel with a certain vacation spirit to it.

Many business visitors to South Florida feel they will have a better time if they check into one of the Miami Beach oceanfront hotels. The Dupont Plaza, with its pool deck and holiday atmosphere, has succeeded in keeping the businessman happy on the mainland. From the lobby, the guest can see the pool deck and watch the yachts go by in the Miami River and across Biscayne Bay. From the cocktail lounge and banquet room on the top floor he can see all of Miami and the blue waters of the Atlantic.

WEEKENDS AT THE COMMERCIAL HOTEL

Incorporating resort features into a commercial hotel has become a nationwide trend in order to combat the sharp drop in weekend occupancy rates. The jet airliner has made it possible for the businessman to get home in a hurry, so you rarely find him staying over at a hotel for the weekend. Harry M. Anholt, president of the Biltmore Hotel in New York, says eighty per cent of his guests now arrive by plane and stay two days. In 1950, they used to come by train and stay twice as long. Roger Sonnabend, head of the hotel division of the Hotel Corporation of America, who says that today's primary guest is the traveling executive, reported:

> He stays for a shorter period of time today. For example, businessmen from the West Coast invariably stayed over the weekend back in 1950. Today, with modern jets, we have few businessmen staying over.

From Nevada came the same answer from Hotel Manager Elliott Mizelle. He says,

> A new occupancy factor in recent years has been the salesman who comes into town for only one day. He used to come in on the weekend and stay a week. The four-engine prop plane cut that stay to four days and now the jet has cut it to one night.

THE SPECIALTY RESTAURANT

One of the answers to the problem of slow weekends for downtown hotels has been the creation of good specialty restaurants and a convivial atmosphere in cocktail lounges. Our first American hotel restaurants were patterned after the European culture: big, heavy dining rooms with a host of waiters at the beck and call of the Maitre de. Then they became more streamlined into a coffee shop type which seemed to fill the gap created by the general opinion that hotel food was not much good anyway. It was certainly common for a hotel guest to get off the elevator and be heard to remark as he and his wife headed for the revolving door, "Where should we eat tonight?"

The specialty restaurant, whether it be the Rib Room, The Luau, or Kingdom of the Sea, is now keeping the guests in the hotel for dinner and is also attracting the town folks. With this type of food operation the hotel achieves quality within the confines of a limited menu. The specialty restaurant has done a great deal to increase the weekend traffic, not only in the restaurant, but in the guestrooms. For there has been an awareness that the new downtown hotels are built for holidays. The Dupont Plaza in Miami has done it with a swimming pool, outdoor dining terrace and elegant cocktail lounges.

ROYAL ORLEANS

In New Orleans, the newest hotel in town is succeeding because it embodies all the charm of the city's French Quarter, plus all the comforts of modern innkeeping. The 350-room Royal Orleans (see illustration, page 37) had to be designed architecturally to conform with the atmosphere of the Quarter. It had to respect the rich background of the site for it was here that the Hotel St. Louis was built in 1838 at a cost of nearly half a million dollars. It burned down three years later, but was rebuilt in an even grander manner. The hotel was the center of social life in New Orleans until the Civil War. It was also one of the South's great slave centers and its 40 feet by 127 feet lobby was brisk marketplace from noon to three o'clock every afternoon. During the era of the carpetbaggers following the Civil War, the hotel became the Louisiana statehouse.

In his book, *The American Hotel*, Jefferson Williamson relates that a Colonel R. J. Rivers bought the building in 1884 and restored it to hoteldom, calling it the Royal. However, he never managed to retrieve its original reputation and the hotel was vacant for many years before it was torn down in 1914. Williamson reminds us that John Galsworthy gave the Royal a place in literature with his description of the hotel in its declining years in *The Inn of Tranquility*.

Today, the Royal Orleans looks out onto the French Quarter and the Mississippi River. Its mullioned arched windows, graceful balconies, and filigree ironwork were designed to meet the strict requirements of the Vieux Carré Commission, a city agency that is the watchdog of all construction in the area. Inside the hotel, the guest is treated to touches of elegance that could be pretentious in almost any other city in the country. The rooftop cafe near the swimming pool is in French style. In one restaurant, dining is by candlelight. In another there are walls of old brick and century-old barn siding. In the hotel are few period reproductions, but many true antiques blended with contemporary furniture. A lot of money was spent on some spectacular French antiques, yet the guestrooms were done on a fairly tight budget. The procedures followed in designing the interiors of Royal Orleans will be examined in Chapter VII.

It seems that there has to be more design emphasis on public spaces

I am convinced there is still a demand for tradition, elegance and fine service.

R. Frederick Woolworth
(Owner of Hotel El Convento, P.R.)

than on the guestrooms today, particularly when dealing with a hotel which, like the Royal Orleans, has special requirements of atmosphere and elegance. Designers of a new hotel no longer have the opportunity to work with an extravagant amount of public space such as was built into hotels like the Plaza or the Waldorf-Astoria. So there must be a great technical knowledge of the hotel's functions in order to use space to better advantage. Certainly we will never see another hotel like the ones that went up in Palm Beach and Boca Raton forty years ago when architects were expected to provide one sitting area after another as places for the guests to take their tea amidst potted palms. The public area of the Royal Orleans is not extensive because it was felt the guests would not do much lobby sitting and people-watching: if they are not in their rooms, they are at the poolside, in the cocktail lounge or one of the restaurants, or out soaking up history and Bourbon Street.

All guestrooms and suites are done in one of three color schemes: monochromatic tones of copper, gold, or pewter. Every room has one wall accented with a textured covering. The walnut furniture is finished in pumice with metal trim and topped with marble.

In providing for a resort atmosphere, Hotel Corporation of America did not overlook today's big convention market. The grand ballroom of the Royal Orleans can be divided into three meeting rooms with a system of theatrical lighting designed to create any mood called for on the agenda or menu. With its convention facilities, its rooftop swimming pool, its elegant atmosphere, and its old world charm, the Royal Orleans has proved an economic as well as an artistic success. Though it is downtown in an old American city, it provides for its guests the same holiday spirit as do the resort hotels examined in the following chapter.

II—HOTELS IN TOWN

Illustrations

The text for this Chapter will be found on pages 9 to 19

MARCO POLO CLUB, WALDORF ASTORIA, NEW YORK N. Y.

Interiors: Donald Deskey Associates; Stanley
    C. Reese, Architect; Russell Heston,
    Designer; Marion E. Landberg,
    Decorator
Photography: Louis Reens

An interesting and profitable idea for a men's
luncheon and dinner club within the confines
of a hotel, the Marco Polo Club at New York
City's Waldorf Astoria has become most successful because of its originality of concept.

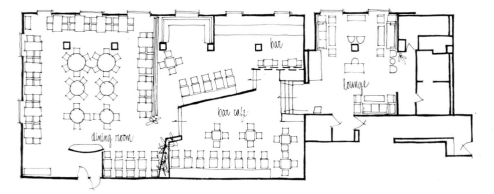

MARCO POLO CLUB, WALDORF ASTORIA, NEW YORK N. Y.

Interiors: Donald Deskey Associates; Stanley
       C. Reese, Architect; Russell Heston,
       Designer; Marion E. Landberg,
       Decorator
Photography: Louis Reens

Right. The diagonal wall of rough plaster to
the left displays tropical plants in staggered
apertures; it also separates this bar-café seating
area from the bar. In the background is the
pièce de resistance of the club: a cathedral wall
10 feet high and 27 feet long with gothic arches,
inspired by the Venetian Palace of Doges.

Below. The massive entrance door offers an imposing welcome. Paneled with dark, roughhewn
squares of hand-rived walnut, it opens to a
direct view of a 6-foot high bronze, copper, and
colored glass sculpture by Edward Chavez.

THE CONRAD HILTON, CHICAGO, ILL.

Architecture: Holabird & Root who also designed the hotel which opened as The Stevens in 1927.

Faced with the loss of large conventions to McCormick Place, the Conrad Hilton Hotel has added 31,000 square feet of exhibition and meeting space. The largest hotel in the world can now boast the most extensive convention facilities.

Above. The International ballroom which will seat 4,000 for meetings and dances and 2,600 for banquets.

Below. A cutaway view of the Hilton Center. On the ground floor level are the Exhibition floor (left) and the Hotel Exhibition Hall; one level up are the Continental Room (to the left) and the Continental lobby; above them are the International ballroom (to the left), its foyer (center), and the Hotel Grand Ballroom (right).

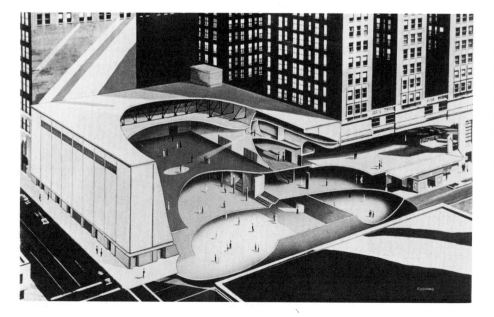

SHERATON-DALLAS, DALLAS, TEX.

Architecture: Welton Becket Associates
Interiors: Mary Morrison Kennedy, A.I.A.,
A.I.D.

Above. You might overlook the clean and un-cluttered registration desk except for the brilliant mural of Venetian glass and marble that is its backdrop. Here in the lobby the columns are black marble and the paneling is teak. To remind its guests they are in Texas, a longhorn design was woven into the rugs.

Right. The 29-story hotel wing of Southland Center is turned to face the wind wall of the 42-story office building. Connecting the two are a shopping arcade at the ground level and a glass enclosed promenade that leads to the second-floor lobby of the hotel.

Facing page. Dramatic staircase connects the ground-level entrance to the lobby of the Sheraton-Dallas Hotel. In the stairwell is a metal and glass stabile by Richard Filipowski that extends to the ceiling of the lobby. The staircase is a steel frame with bold concrete supports.

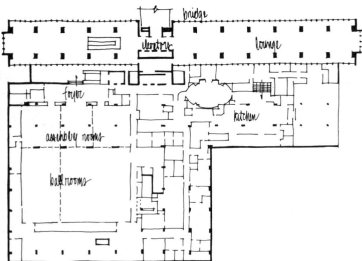

DENVER HILTON,
DENVER, COLO.

Architecture: I. M. Pei Associates; Rogers & Butler, Associated Architects; William B. Tabler, Consultant Architect

Photography: George Cserna

Above right. Monumental is the only word to describe the 21-story Hilton Hotel in Denver's Mile High Center.

Above left. The grille of the hotel is broken only once by a second-level tunnel of Plexiglas to the department store across the street (visible in the picture to the right). This view is of the entrance to the tunnel from the second floor lobby.

Left. Plan of the lobby floor of the second level of the Denver Hilton.

Right. This lobby area of the Denver Hilton is truly fine art, but who can be sure that it makes the hotel guest comfortable? The gold tree sculpture by Harry Bertoia, growing from the terrazzo floor, contributes to the coldness of the hotel's public spaces. What texture there is in this area is contributed by the jeweled plastic ceiling designed by Alexander Girard.

DENVER HILTON,

Left. The cocktail lounge separates the lounge from the bar and is enclosed by parapets.

Above. The architectural press did not think much of the guest room designed by Elliott Frey & Associates of Hilton. This room was criticized for its "mail-order taste," but it is far warmer than the model room suggested by the architect.

Left. View along the Plexiglas tunnel (see previous page) from the hotel lobby to the department store across the street.

Facing page. The main lobby contains a lounge, cocktail lounge, and bar. A Bertoia sculpture representing the Colorado state flower (the Columbine) hangs above the oval bar with its backless stools.

DUPONT PLAZA CENTER, MIAMI, FLA.

Architecture: John Petersen & Frank Shuflin
Interiors: Henry End Associates
Photography: Alexandre Georges

Above. Stretching 575 feet along the Miami River where it flows into Biscayne Bay is the Dupont Plaza Center, a unique structure combining a 250-room hotel, office building, and an architect's sample bureau. The 12-story structure is faced with panels of aluminum in a variety of colors.

Below. Schematic plan shows the relationship of the building's many functions.

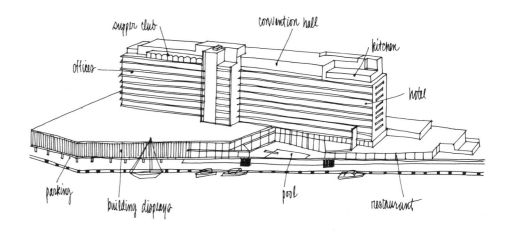

EXECUTIVE HOUSE, CHICAGO, ILL.

Architecture: Milton M. Schwartz & Associates
Interiors: Lapidus, Kornblath, Harle & O'Mara

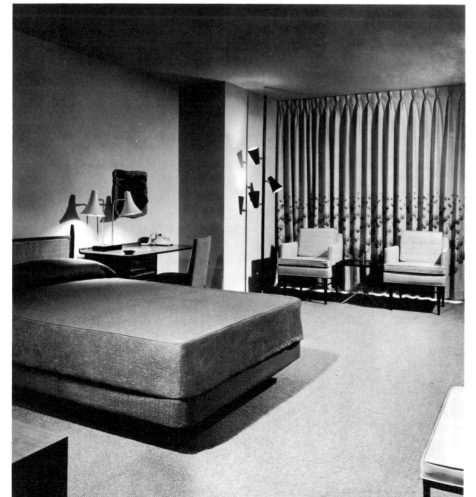

Executive House in the Chicago Loop (see page 8) appears to be the only structure lucky enough to catch the setting sun. Completed in 1958, its 40 floors make it the tallest reinforced concrete structure in the country.

Above. Studio apartment in the Executive House measures 12½ x 20 feet and with a ceiling height of eight feet. Originally designed as an apartment hotel, the interiors have a home-like atmosphere and each apartment has a small kitchen and bar.

SUMMIT HOTEL,
NEW YORK, N. Y.

Architecture: Morris Lapidus, A.I.A., A.I.D.,
N.S.I.D.
Photography: Gottscho-Schleisner

Right. The Summit, with less than 100 feet of frontage on Lexington Avenue, has a serpentine facade. Pressed to achieve a hotel of 800 rooms on such a site, it is remarkable that the architect came off as well as he did.

Below. There's a variety of design in the elevator lobby with the doors faced with porcelain enamel; the far wall a bronze and glass mural lighted from behind. Between the elevator doors with their abstract designs in green, turquoise, and black are sections of smoked mirror wall.

Top, facing page. The lobby seating area is here defined by a multicolored rug of blues and greens (it was later removed in a general toning-down effort at the behest of the owners). Ceiling design of interlocking aluminum rings of white and gold was designed to stretch visually the limited space of the lobby. Columns are faced with plywood stripped with metal.

Bottom, facing page. Multitudes of materials and Latin American themes are joined in the Summit's Gaucho Room which adjoins the lobby. Ceiling beams are crusted with cattle brands and the lighting fixtures are in the form of steer heads. Colors of saffron brown, gold, and olive are picked up from the carpet which has an inlaid pegged plank pattern. Armchairs are covered with burnt orange leather.

Above. Wooden bead curtain serves as the back-drop for a Carioca Lounge banquette which is framed with mosaic tile. Table tops are transparent brown over yellow porcelain enamel.

PITTSBURGH HILTON, PITTSBURGH, PA.

Architecture: William B. Tabler
Interiors: Ernest Wottitz, A.I.D. and David T.
        Williams, A.I.D.
Photography: lobby, James Vincent

Above. Handsomest aspect of the Pittsburgh Hilton is the clean line of the exterior with its walls of aluminum and glass. The 24-story building with 807 guest rooms faces Commonwealth Center in the city's Gateway Center.

Upper right. Mechanical functions of the ceiling hardware are all to evident in the mezzanine lobby that leads to the grand ballroom. Columns here are covered with travertine marble and the far wall is teak paneling.

Lower right. The immense ballroom of the Pittsburgh Hilton can accommodate a banquet for 2,000 and a meeting of 2,500. Soundproof partitions can divide the room into four areas. Walls are covered with gold plastic and the chairs are covered in antique white.

ROYAL YORK HOTEL, TORONTO, CANADA

Architecture: Ross, Fish, Duschenes & Barrett
Interiors: Ernest G. H. Rex, I.D.S., A.I.D.
Photography: Canadian Pacific Photos

Above. Lighter colored section of the exterior is a 17-story addition to the Royal York. This brought the total rooms to 1,600, making it the largest hotel in Canada.

Right top and center. The flavor is national in the new interiors of the $10 million addition to the Royal York Hotel. The geometric figures of the luminous canopies and floor of the 180x80 foot Canadian Room suggest a native handicraft. The ceiling lighting is made of gold, silver, and blue panels. It is one of many cases in the hotel where architect and designer have used lighting and materials to dramatize space. The long walls are faced with strips of poplar fronting and acoustical blanket. The end walls are draped with a fabric that incorporates the elements of the Canadian coat-of-arms.

Lower right. Paneled in pine — Quebec Room. Chandeliers are Flemish-French. Oil mural by L. Smith is of colonial days in Quebec.

36

In the heart of the French Quarter, the Royal Orleans Hotel captures the romance of the historic city. Working strictly within the regulations of the Vieux Carré Commission which guards the architecture of the French Quarter, Curtis & Davis achieved a handsome building that does honor to the site. It was here in 1838 that the Hotel St. Louis was built, the social center of New Orleans until the Civil War. Fluted cast iron columns march grandly down the narrow sidewalk in support of the balconies with their filigree grillework.

THE ROYAL ORLEANS, NEW ORLEANS, LA.

Architecture: Curtis & Davis; Koch & Wilson, Associates
Interiors: Henry End Associates
Photography: Frank Lotz Miller, Ezra Stoller

Above. Sliding panels of wrought iron separate the lounge from the Esplanade dining room. Dominating the area is a mural map of old New Orleans done in sepia tones and gold leaf. The artist is Shirley Tatterfield. Table tops are white marble and the chair upholstery alternates white leather and citron velvet. Carpeting is citron, melon, and gray-green.

THE ROYAL ORLEANS

Left. One of the special suites of the Royal Orleans provides a rooftop view of the city. The room is done in tones of pewter with accents of Thai silk in the sofa pillows.

Right. Wood from a century-old barn was used for the paneling in the Rib Room of the Royal Orleans. Combined with old brick, it makes an appropriate background for the men-only atmosphere at lunch. The ladies are invited to dine by hurricane lamplight in the evening. Beamed ceiling is antique charcoal and the flooring is slate. Chairs are upholstered in black leather and the table linen is white with an overlay of brilliant crimson.

Left. Roofscape of the Royal Orleans provides guests with a sheltered swimming pool and lounge deck, plus a horizon view of the city. Beyond the sundeck umbrellas is La Riviera dining room.

Right. Curtains of shocking pink and crimson guard the socializing in the street-level bar from the gaze of passersby. Antique lanterns flanking the bar lend a historical note. Cocktail chairs are covered in black as is the leather bar rail. Flooring here is slate. This bar can be entered from the upstairs lounge shown at the rear or from the adjoining Rib Room .

ST. ANTHONY HOTEL, SAN ANTONIO, TEXAS

Interiors: styled and designed by Dorothy
     Draper & Co., Inc.

The distinctive lightness and dramatic scale of
a Dorothy Draper interior is evident in this
dining room of the St. Anthony Hotel.

III—RESORT HOTELS

It used to be easy to tell the difference between hotels. The resort hotels had big porches, wicker furniture, chintz curtains, and three huge meals a day. The commercial hotels had leather furniture in the lobby, bad food in the dining room, and dirty carpets in the bedrooms.

Today, the only real difference is in location. The new hotels going up in New York and San Francisco offer the guest the same cheerful atmosphere as the ones in Puerto Rico, Nassau, and Hawaii.

The businessman at a convention in Chicago expects to find the same standards of comfort and excitement as he did the week before on vacation in Nassau or Bermuda. Somebody once said that the only way to tell the difference between the resort hotel and the new commercial hotel was that one had a balcony and the other had venetian blinds and permanently locked windows. But that definition has had to be discarded because new in-town hotels began to include balconies to provide the guest with a vacation atmosphere.

Speaking to a hotel management workshop at Cornell University, the travel editor of *The New York Times* once said a resort hotel must have atmosphere, warmth, and a personality that is distinctive and unique. Paul Friedlander added that,

> Of two resorts, one is busy, brisk, big, and brittle. The other is busy, big, warm, and intimate. I will return to the second one because it has "gemütlichkeit."

THE CHANGING VACATION

He was absolutely right, but today this does not hold true only for the resort hotel. Yet there is a special place for the resort in the story of the hotel industry. In the early days, it was bound up with the development of the exclusive spa, the mountain camps, the boardwalk of Atlantic City, and the architectural bouillabaisse of Miami Beach. In each case, there was a hard lesson to be learned from the effects of an expanding economy and faster airplanes. People with more money want to go farther. Vacations are a symbol of status and when the secretary can go away for two weeks to the mountains, her boss must look for another place to play and rest.

In the decade following World War II it was Miami Beach in the winter. At Christmas the family arrived aboard the Sunshine Special with two or three trunks and checked into a hotel for the "season." This affluent

Those who talk about playing down to a vulgar level to appeal to a great number of people don't really believe what they are saying. It is more likely true that they don't have good taste themselves and really don't know how to do the job better. Could Leonard Bernstein write a banal tune unless it were a complete spoof?

Henry End, A.I.D., I.D.I.

segment of society returned north en masse with the last running of the ponies at Hialeah Race Course. Hotel men turned off the lights, locked the doors, and went on vacation themselves. But then came the four-engine plane that could carry eighty passengers from New York to Miami in little over four hours. And on the drawing boards were plans for the jet liner that could increase the capacity by fifty per cent and cut the time in half. Because airlines cannot economically close down flights for the summertime, they promoted the summertime budget vacation in Florida. Those planeloads of secretaries, factory workers, and just plain folks uncorked the greatest hotel building boom in history. In the decade up to 1958, there were more hotel rooms built along the five-mile strip of oceanfront in Miami Beach than in the rest of the world put together. And in the rush to outdo the competition, taste went out the window and vulgarity became the order of the day. "This year's hotel" had to produce louder "Ohs and Ahs" or the owner felt cheated.

When economics and the lure of newer resorts in the Caribbean killed off the hotel building spree, Miami Beach could count 30,000 hotel rooms, plus an additional 27,000 apartment units.

It was the combination of a cold winter in 1958, coupled with the national economic recession, that uncovered the bitter truth about the world's greatest resort. The hotels, each one noisier than the next, had been built as speculative ventures by people who knew nothing about the business. So long as the postwar boom lasted, Miami Beach was in great shape: mortgages piled atop mortgages as the pink and blue stucco palaces were leased and leased again; the hotel room was a commodity to be traded. But with the decline in tourists came the realization that most of the new hotels had been so badly designed that they were virtually impossible to operate profitably at anything less than near-capacity. Morris Lapidus, the architect whose name is so closely tied to the image of Miami Beach flamboyance, has estimated that half the hotels in that resort were designed by and for people with no prior experience in the business.

While one might fail to find a common ground of taste and design with Lapidus, it must nevertheless be said that the hotels he designs "work" well for the management. If their Americana Hotel in Florida had not been successful, Larry and Bob Tisch would presumably not have hired Lapidus to design the Loew's hotels in New York and Puerto Rico. But as we saw at the Summit in New York (discussed on page 12), there is a limit to how much stimulation you can give a hotel guest. It is all a question of degree. According to Lapidus:

> People want hotels to be places of excitement. They are not looking for a home away from home. Why do they go to the movies or watch television? They want to see a more glamorous way of life. They want to escape from their own four walls.

But this is no reason to make a hotel, whether it be in San Juan or in downtown New York, so glamorous and overwhelming that the guest feels uncomfortable. People are living more informally, more casually today. They look to do this in hotel surroundings, too.

There are two basic theories of hotel design. One is that the hotel

44

should provide a complete change from the home atmosphere and should be a place of glamour and excitement for the traveler. The other is that it should be a home away from home with a general elevation of taste in home decor. There is every reason to think that the latter theory is a sound one and that flashy and jazzy effects in hotel lobbies and guestrooms are a mistake.

THE SEVILLE

Many fine examples of good interiors in resort hotels lie ahead in these pages, but it might be just as well to make a confession right now. While today I stand firmly opposed to the ostentation represented in so many hotel interiors, there is in Miami Beach a hotel that hangs around my neck like an albatross. It can serve as a lesson for all designers under pressure from inexperienced management. The hotel is the Seville, an example of how bad a job can get when a designer goes along with every suggestion from the owner because he has been successful in other types of business ventures. Money can be a great persuader, but also a great corrupter.

The Fontainebleau had opened the year before and, while I was not convinced that this was the kind of hotel Miami Beach needed, the developers of the Seville felt they needed something that would outshine last year's hotel. Starting with the selection of the name, the Seville was doomed to pretentiousness. But I was green and this was my first major hotel in a resort area. Too eager to please, I found myself using all sorts of imitative gimmicks in an effort to carry off the Spanish kick. Maybe it all can be blamed on the cha-cha-cha and mambo craze that swept in from the Caribbean in the early 1950s. But whatever the reason, this was the owner's "bent" and I went along.

It is at that early stage of concept that the designer must stop and consider, when he must dig in and fight for what he thinks is right. The designers, not the owners, are the taste makers. The owner comes to the designer in search of an image for his hotel, his store, or his restaurant. Often he arrives with a notion that carries with it the threat of fakery and bad taste. It is then that the designer must pull him back to the heart of the program and pick a better direction. When a designer is employed to do a good job, he should explain that he must do a good job not only for the client, but for himself as well.

The developer of a 300-room hotel would never consider himself capable of working out the structural engineering or the mechanics of air-conditioning. But the same considerations do not keep his wife or daughter-in-law from thinking she knows how it should be decorated. The businessman usually gets so caught up with the headaches of financing and construction, that his wife will often become frustrated at not being part of this great venture. Let the designer beware the sight of Mrs. Owner on the job because it is often the sign that her husband is going to allow her to putter with the hotel decor for appeasement's sake. She has been reading all the magazines and maybe she went through the Merchandise Mart on a tour. All her friends exclaimed over the decorating she did in the penthouse or the cottage at Cape Cod.

It was in the public spaces that the owner's interference hurt the most at the Seville. The gold wall tile, the sham silk on the furniture, and the supplicating maidens in the lobby center all added up to a dismal failure. Because of the attempted lavishness, the hotel wound up with a lobby that was much too large. In the guestrooms, things went better. The furnishings were designed en masse so the factor of economy prevented too many mistakes. But even here, especially in the suites, some things were overdone: I recall one fuchsia pink wall covered with matador prints!

New owners of the Seville revamped the public spaces in an attempt to make them more functional, but too much was basically wrong. It was simply a case of the architect and the designer spending all their time pleasing the owner. Nor could one put the blame on any special efforts to save money. The owner, of course, was looking for the most for the least, but in that respect it was no different from most jobs. All developers want more space for less money, but on the other hand the finest design work has not always been done with a high budget; good taste and design are not necessarily related to cost. My fee was not a large one, but I was anxious to get the job. Overanxious would be more like it. It is a mistake I have never repeated and it can be a lesson to others. It is better to wait for the right kind of big assignment because there is nothing worse than a big failure.

CARIBE HILTON

To turn now to a hotel that might have changed the course of architecture and taste in Miami Beach had it been built there instead of in Puerto Rico. The Caribe Hilton of San Juan (see illustrations, page 61) was designed in the late 1940s for the American tourist on vacation. It is luxurious without being gaudy. An early example of international resort architecture, it retains today a freshness that makes it competitive with the newest hotels on the island.

In 1950, *Architectural Forum* said of the Caribe Hilton that it had

the color, texture, and finish demanded by Americans off to the semi-tropics — an atmosphere of relaxed daytime sunniness and at night, drama dissipating out into a big southern sky. And constant obvious luxury.

The cynicism of the journalist shows in his doubts concerning the tourist's ability to recognize that the luxurious atmosphere was achieved without pretentious and posh decorating. Those doubts must have been laid to rest when a few years later, a 100-room wing was added. Said *Forum:*

The primary success and architectural lesson in this structure is that such a building can be lavish and still retain a comfortable human scale. The Caribe Hilton has a very large area of public space for its 350 rooms — two entire public floors. But space is spread horizontally, not shot away in lofty high ceilinged spaces for the conventionally impressionable.

That is a wonderful phrase . . . "conventionally impressionable." It sums up the fault that lies at the heart of the problem Miami Beach faces in its middle years. The conservative person is made uneasy by a concentration of lavishness that has no lasting quality. The very goal of building "this year's hotel" in Miami Beach had within it the seeds of obsolescence and self-destruction. The Caribe Hilton, on the other hand, retained its charm a dozen years after the doors opened. What is more, it set off a chain reaction that produced Hilton hotels around the world. It was also one of the first major successes of "Operation Bootstrap", the program established by Puerto Rico to pull the island up from poverty through the development of industry.

In the immediate postwar era, the government's Puerto Rico Development Company wrote to a half dozen American hotel men asking about the possibility of a partnership. Puerto Rico would supply the money to put up a building if the hotel man would furnish and operate it. Conrad Hilton wrote back in the courtly Spanish he had learned in his early days in the southwest. He addressed the letter, "Estimados Amigos". It is not known whether any of the other hotel men even replied, but not only did the San Juan government build the hotel, but Hilton persuaded them to furnish it also. His program was that the Caribe Hilton should belong solely to the island; that the Hilton organization would come in with operating capital, architectural consultants, and managerial controls; he promised to hire Puerto Ricans for most of the staff and to institute a training program for them within the Hilton chain in the United States.

The government in San Juan was easier to convince than the directors of the Hilton chain. In his book, *Be My Guest*, Hilton recalled the impassioned speech he made to the board after Puerto Rico had agreed to put up seven million dollars to build the hotel:

> The world is shrinking, what used to be a month-long vacation trip is now almost a weekend possibility. Businessmen can cover far-off territories. The airplane is here to stay. Americans not only can, but want to travel farther, see more, do more in less time. This is progress and the hotel business must progress right with it. Father Junipero set his California missions a day's journey apart. Today you can fly over the whole string in a few hours. If we are to set out hotels a day's journey apart, we'd be around the world in no time. So perfectly sound business is in line with national idealism.

The board was not completely sold on the idea, but did agree to put up a limited amount of money to get a new company started. That was the beginning of Hilton Hotels International and the slogan of the parent firm was changed from "Across the Nation" to "Around the World."

The Caribe Hilton not only made money for the government, it also served as a symbol of the island's industrial revolution. The businessman flying into San Juan could not help but be impressed by the sight of that striking building overlooking the sea. The comfort he enjoyed in his room in that building added to an awareness that this was no sloppy banana republic, but an island determined to go first class.

As a forerunner of the resort industry in the islands, it is interesting to consider the evolution of the studio room in the Caribe Hilton. This was a postwar phenomena and an attempt to provide more living area in hotel bedrooms. The designer is never asked how big a guestroom should be.

Whereas resort hotels tended to be rather unbusinesslike propositions before the war, run by gregarious Ma's and Pa's with only the foggiest notions about scientific management, the postwar years have produced a breed of businesslike operators who know exactly how to apply cost-accounting procedures, know how to take advantage of the tax laws, and not the least, have a flair for promotion.

Fortune Magazine

Its size usually is determined by the structural engineering and the effort to find space for as many beds as possible.

As rooms became smaller in new hotels, the studio bed appeared to be the answer to the space problem — it seemed the best way to provide the kind of space needed for such things as impromptu business meetings and private parties without the awkwardness of having to sit all over the beds. Two studio beds in a room did not detract from its living-room air. At the same time, since no hotel room should be a simple room, the studio bed was economical, fitting as it does into the smallest of rooms. For several years the studio bed seemed to be the right approach, but eventually it became evident that psychologically it was a failure. No matter how good the equipment, whether or not the finest mattress is used, the guest feels he is being forced to sleep on a sofa instead of a real bed. The other difficulty lies in housekeeping: the studio bed has to be made up in the early evening.

At the Caribe Hilton, guestrooms are of generous size and the studio beds are used to give the living-room appearance. However, in the new wing and in redesigned rooms, there has been a switch to twin beds. The trend in resort hotels seems to be towards a conventional bedroom layout, particularly when the clientele is above middle-age. This group of tourists wants a substantial bed.

After a day on the golf course or at the pool, the guest wants to nap before dinner. Care must be taken in the choice of materials for bedspreads, upholstery, and wall coverings because of suntan oils. Plastics are not the only solution, however. Washability and durability seem to be the answers to this problem.

La CONCHA

Toro and Ferrer of Puerto Rico, architects for the Hilton hotel, also designed the 250-room La Concha Hotel in one of San Juan's better residential areas overlooking the Caribbean (see illustrations, page 62). As clean and uncluttered as the Caribe Hilton, this newer resort has exciting elements. The name of the hotel (Spanish for shell) gave rise to the dramatic architectural form of the supper club. The concrete roof is folded in the shape of a limpet shell and dips gracefully to ground, but still provides a view of the oceanside pool. The carpeting is sand colored with a pattern of sea urchin. How much more fitting than the Greek columns and Roman statuary that clutter up the lobbies in Miami Beach. Of La Concha, *Interiors* editor Olga Gueft wrote:

> The concrete shell which roofs its supper club is not merely poetic as a concept and handsome as a sculptural counterpoint to the architectural complex of the hotel, but also provides a wonderful and strange interior which lends itself to dramatic lighting and affords vistas of the transparent deep blue Caribbean in three directions from the glass windows that join the pool with the lower edges of the shell.

As in the Caribe Hilton, the lobby of La Concha is open to the trade winds sweeping in from the southeast. It serves to remind the guest he is in the tropics and can enjoy it. In too many resort hotels, public areas are completely divorced by concrete and draperies from the natural environment. Nature is brought into the lobby of La Concha through a water garden that is open to the sky. Along one long wall behind the pool is a sand and concrete mural by George Nocito and Bert Schwartz. Its texture, plus a great expanse of teak paneling, gives the lobby warmth contrasted to the concrete grid of the twelve-story guestroom tower.

RIVIERA AND HABANA HILTON

Though they are both now hidden behind Fidel Castro's sovietized "sugar curtain," two Havana hotels merit space in this chapter. They are the Riviera, designed by Polevitzky-Johnson Associates of Miami, and the Habana Hilton by Welton Becket and Associates of Los Angeles.

It is interesting to note that the 24 million dollar Hilton hotel, with thirty stories containing 630 rooms, was financed by the Cuban restaurant workers union. So Conrad Hilton was actually working for his employees and he had more trouble with that hotel than with any of his others. It was perhaps because of the independent attitude adopted by the employees of the Habana Hilton. Although they must have realized that good service would help to assure a successful operation and therefore a bigger return on their investment, Hilton found that many of the staff were only too well aware that this was their hotel and felt that both management and guests must be constantly reminded of the fact. However, all that is history. Today the hotel is called the Havana Libre and nobody is paying thirty Yankee dollars a day for the rooms overlooking Morro Castle.

Yet the hotel created for Hilton in Havana will go down in design annals as a high mark in the collaboration of sterling architecture and native craftsmanship (see illustrations, page 63). There were great spaces, but all of them were treated warmly. The lobby was designed in the manner of a traditional Cuban garden patio and there were full grown trees beneath a plastic dome studded with clear bubbles to admit the sunshine. The luxuriant plantings graced a background of four colorful kinds of Cuban marble on the floors and walls.

The social life of the hotel was centered on the second floor, but one of the features of the lobby level was El Patio Bar, a fanciful version of the sidewalk saloons so familiar to pre-Castro visitors in Havana. This was no Sloppy Joe's, but it achieved that same feeling of openness through the use of wrought iron grillework. The ceiling was playfully done in green and blue striped canvas and behind the bar was a textured pattern of mahogany and cane.

A cantilevered staircase led the guest from the garden atmosphere of the lobby to the more sophisticated level where the roulette wheels spun and the cocktail lounge was tuned to the lively shaking of the daiquiri makers. From the bar, the guest looked out to the bright orange and pink cabanas and the pool deck of native travertine.

In its collaboration with the Cuban art world, the Becket design staff outdid the standard established at Cairo. Everywhere one looked, there were examples of top-flight creative talent, from the nine-ton mosaic tile mural across the front entrance to the ceramic tile table tops used on the guestroom balconies.

The designs for rugs were taken from the work of outstanding Cuban artists, as was the layout of the garden walk that overlooked the pool. Landscape architects used tiles, stone and plants to follow the pattern of a painting by Luis Martinex Pedro, the first known example of such an artist-landscaper partnership in creativity. The facade mural by Amelia Palaez was fashioned in Venice of sixteen million pieces of Italian glass mosaic tile; the design, in black, white and blue, is of native fruits and flowers. Also on the outside of the building is an abstract seascape by Cundo Bermudez. Another outstanding example of this collaboration of architect and artist was the dramatic ten-panel tile mural created for the cocktail lounge by Rene Portocarrero whose paintings can be found at the Museum of Modern Art in New York and in many of the world's private collections. Several of Portocarrero's paintings were used in the suites.

The list of art credits for the Habana Hilton is endless, but attention must also be paid to the layout of guestrooms, which was particularly good. Twin bedrooms adjoined studio rooms for alternative use as suites. Becket used a sliding screen of pierced composition board derived from sugar cane to divide the dressing area from the main part of the room. Beneath the dressing table was a storage chest; it was not large, but ample for the tourists who arrived with most of their clothing in garment bags ready for hanging in the five-foot closet. The beds were set back from sliding glass doors that led to a large balcony furnished with lounges and rattan chairs. The efficient layout of the dressing room and bathroom provided a great expanse of living area in the guestroom. Even in the rooms fitted with twin beds, the headboards were kept low to achieve the effect of lounges. In the adjoining studio room, Becket used a convertible sofa and a daybed cornered to a table that incorporated pillow storage, telephone, radio, and a maid call system.

The finish of the furniture was mahogany and tops of tables and desks were laminated plastic. While the attitude of the Hilton staff might not have been too solicitous of the Yankee guests, it would be interesting to know what they think of the Chinese Communists who were invited by Senor Castro to help create a worker's paradise. The Chinese are said to have imported their own version of the American plan and arrived with charcoal burners to cook meals in the hotel rooms. It meant the end of the mica finish on all the tables, desks, and dressing counters.

While the Habana Hilton represented a hands-across-the-sea program of American business enterprise, the Havana Riviera was an export that combined the luxury of Miami Beach with the crap-shooting know-how of Las Vegas. At the Hilton hotel, the casino had to be sought out on the second floor. At the Riviera, it was right there at the lobby entrance and difficult to by-pass.

The Habana Hilton and the Riviera were both designed to attract the American tourists concentrated 200 miles away in South Florida. The hotels were counted upon to aid the Cuban treasury, but they were not designed to cater to the citizens of that country.

Yet the Riviera (see illustrations, page 63) was more attuned to the resort atmosphere. The leggy nineteen-story guestroom tower stands back from La Malecon that in pre-Castro days carried a steady stream of shiny new cars from downtown Havana to the exclusive Vedado section. The site, on a slight rise, overlooks the sea and most of the 400 rooms have the benefit of that view.

The main lobby is low-scaled, stretching from the entrance through to the pool deck and cabanas. There were stores and coffee shop on the lower level. The vacationer arriving at the Riviera did not have to consult a brochure in his room to learn about the hotel's fun-making facilities. On the walk across marble from front door to elevator, the guest passed by the casino and cabaret first, then the cocktail lounge and main dining room. What better way to put him in a holiday mood than the sounds of the soft gallop of dice mixed with the merry clinking of glasses, the strumming of guitars, and the whirring of the roulette wheel?

For their architect, the developers of the Riviera selected a man who had demonstrated his skill in designing for a resort area without pretentiousness and vulgarity. Igor Polevitzky designed the Shelbourne Hotel in Miami Beach in the immediate postwar era and the pity is that it was not used as a model for the hotels that came along in the decade that followed.

Albert Parvin and Company of Los Angeles was brought into the job early and an office was set up in Miami to correlate the interiors with the architectural design. As was done by Welton Becket's staff in the case of the Nile Hilton, the Parvin designers started first with a research program, in this case at the Havana Art Museum. From there came the information for the local color built into the Riviera. Backgrounds of terrazzo, tile, and marble were held down to white and off-whites to accentuate the boldness of Cuban art work. One of the most outstanding of these was Enzo Gallo's abstract frieze on the wall that gracefully turned the guest from the lobby into the gaming room.

It was said of the Riviera that, while Miami-styled, it bore traces of Latin influence in the "emphasis on sparkling, padded sumptuosity." Two correct adjectives and an appropriate noun, but it might have been added the hotel succeeded so well because the architect and designer never crossed that line to over-stimulation which gave such a transitory lavishness to so many Florida hotels.

THE FONTAINEBLEAU

In discussing such lavishness, the start must be made with the Fontainebleau, the 20th century oceanfront coliseum that replaced the Firestone estate in Miami Beach at the height of the hotel boom. Dozens of hotels had preceded it along Collins Avenue, each one more flamboyant than the next. But the great 14-story curving wall of the Fontainebleau, its 17,000 square feet of marble-sheathed lobby, its statuary and its "French renaissance" style were the high-water mark. It can be observed today that the hotels that followed, and there were some big ones, never went so far in trying to overwhelm the visitor with such a show of grandeur.

The architect, Morris Lapidus, also designs the interiors of his hotels and in the case of the Fontainebleau he had a thirteen-million dollar budget for a 564-room hotel. He has been damned by architectural and design critics for his flamboyance but Lapidus has this to say about his Fontainebleau job:

I've given these people something to gape at. You might call it a tasteful three-ring circus. . . . I gave it the luxurious once-over where it shows. If I put the money in there, you saw it and you can be sure everyone else will too. . . . I think I've struck something. Everyone likes this hotel. We've let man's primitive desire for decoration come out — and brought it up to his cultural level.

The statement speaks for itself. It was always the architect's contention that the Fontainebleau resulted from the owner's choice of the hotel name and his insistence on French decoration. But let Lapidus tell it in his own words as recorded by *Interiors* magazine when the hotel opened:

We took renaissance forms, cleaned them up and much to our surprise found they didn't clash with modern. Take the wall over the reception desk. You might describe it as floating panels of teak and gold against a white background. If those were really renaissance panels, they'd probably have a complicated curving outline. We simplified it and to lighten the wall, we floated the panels on white Formica. In a renaissance palace you'd find a white marble floor with a pattern of small black diamond-shaped keys. We changed the shape and then we gave it a sweeping curve you'd never find in the renaissance.

Referring to the design background for the suspended staircase leading to the mezzanine, Lapidus said,

Instead of a brocade, we blew up a Piranesi print. Instead of marble balusters, we designed little gold ones. The form and richness come from the renaissance, but the feeling is contemporary. Underneath, just for fun, we put a marble pool.

The lobby was filled with good French antiques that were stripped and refinished in gold and white. Lamps were made from blackamoors and bisque figurines. Wherever the guest turned, he could find cherubs, a gilded wood escutcheon, cupid-topped French clocks, dripping crystal. It was always more and more until the effect was crushing for anyone with a modicum of taste.

Not only does Lapidus feel he had given the public what it wants, but also that the owner had been satisfied. As one of the leaders of a panel discussion held by the "Miami Herald" to take the pulse of the hotel industry in 1962, Lapidus said this of the Fontainebleau:

It was designed for a certain type of person. I don't like it personally, but they do. The owner says, "My guests are very rich people who love rich, lavish surroundings." So you play up to the client's client. I certainly am not designing the hotel for myself and not even for the owner, really. He tells me what he wants because he knows who his customers are.

With all the cherubs and chandeliers, the Lapidus firm built into the Fontainebleau the things that were to save it when the economy of Miami Beach was forced to switch gears from a vacationland for the very wealthy to a major convention city. The Fontainebleau had six kitchens that could put out 3,000 meals in ten dining rooms. The ballroom and the fancy dining hall were so related that the dividing wall folded back to provide seating for 3,000 auditorium style or banquet seating for 2,000.

The client's level, intellectual and artistic, is a factor in every kind of interior, whether commercial or public, or private and residential — for it takes a knowing client to hire a good designer. The best interiors we see are those done by able and sensitive designers for clients whose taste is not merely good, but rather sympathetic to the idiom of the designer. Such interiors are not found often, but when they are, they look alive. They convince and gladden the eye.

Olga Gueft, Editor
Interiors

These facts helped in the transition period of 1960 during which owner Ben Novack spent ten million dollars to make the Fontainebleau a convention resort. A new fourteen-story wing went up and between this monolithic slab and the 350-foot curve of the original building went a million-dollar kitchen to serve a giant convention hall capable of seating 8,000 and feeding 5,000. With 1,032 rooms, Novack was now prepared to meet the challenge of the Americana Hotel in neighboring Bal Harbour. This is the one Lapidus designed for the Tisch brothers who learned the business from their parents in Atlantic City. It must be noted in passing that for his addition to the Fontainebleau, Novack did not return to the Lapidus office. The story that echoed up and down Miami Beach was that Novack felt the architect had demonstrated some sort of disloyalty in designing the Eden Roc Hotel that went up next door to the Fontainebleau the following year. The resentment was fed by comment that the smaller Eden Roc (350 rooms) represented a higher degree of elegance. And the burn reached deeper a year later when the Tisch family opened with a seventeen million dollar news-making salute to the republics of the Americas.

The Americana came along just at the moment when the South Florida economy did its turnabout to the convention trade. The hotel was not designed especially for this kind of catering, but the Tisch brothers realized two months after opening day that their 475 excellent guestrooms and lanai suites could not be filled year-round with vacationers. Fortunately, and unlike the older hotels of Miami Beach jammed into 50- and 100-foot sites, the Americana had the room to build. The garage was quickly converted into a banquet room and work started on an exhibition hall. Within two years, the hotel was expanded to 780 rooms and the convention sales force was larger than the one for the whole city of Miami Beach.

Charles Craddock, Director of the Americana in Bal Harbour, said convention trade in 1962 represented 76% of income. During the hotel conference sponsored by the "Miami Herald," Craddock revealed some statistics that give an indication of what can be done by sound management, strong promotion, and topflight hotel service. The hotel grossed twelve million dollars in 1961, one million derived from its supper club. The hotel has 1,000 employees and a payroll of $2,500,000. To achieve that gross, the hotel spent $600,000 on advertising and promotion — almost double the usual percentage. In the peak of the winter season, the Americana runs 85% to 90% occupancy when the European rate is $35 double. In the medium months occupancy drops to 70% to 75% and in mid-summer down to 45%.

Craddock estimates that the average American-plan conventioneer checks in for four and a half days and spends $50 a day while the European-plan guest spends about $40. In 1962, the Americana nailed down one out of four conventions in the area and could count bookings ahead as far as 1970. There were 197 conventions booked at the Americana during 1962, representing 236,250 guest days. And of that impressive total, 63% was repeat business.

Here again, Lapidus created a functional and successful hotel at the same time he was piling into it an excess of color and adornment. The Americana (see illustrations, page 67) is the best of his designs in Florida. Swirling black and white mosaic floors that resemble the pavements of Rio de Janeiro fit better into a Florida hotel than do those cherubs and marble-topped antiques of the Fontainebleau and Eden Roc. So do the Indian symbols in the enamel murals done by Charles Jacobson, the leather wall tiles in the Gaucho steak house, and the stainless steel sculpture at the lobby entrance.

The 160-foot-long lobby is separated into two tiers, which separate the incoming and outgoing guests from the milling of convention delegates. Dividing the two areas is a colorful screen of Inca-inspired carvings by Herman Brockdorf. The real eye-catcher in the lobby is a forty-foot-high terrarium open to the sky. Behind its glass walls are full-grown tropical trees growing from orchid-festooned boulders. The guests circle this man-made forest on their way to the ground-level stores, steak house, and coffee shop.

Lapidus is always at his best in the layout of guestrooms and bathrooms, and in this respect the Americana is particularly well planned. The lanai suites provide the big spender with a terrace and a living room, plus a bedroom that can be screened with a folding door. There is also a serving pantry tucked away near the entrance to the suite.

ARUBA CARIBBEAN

Perhaps the best hotel job to come out of the Lapidus office was the Aruba Caribbean in the Dutch West Indies, off the coast of Venezuela (see illustrations, page 68). Here there was sympathetic and thoughtful use of native materials to make the 140-room hotel fit the scene. The hotel stands off the ground on stilts to catch the trade winds and the lobby and public rooms are gathered on the in-shore side of the hotel. The lobby is a handsome one, not as overstated as one would expect after seeing this architect's work in Florida. The cement tile lobby floor creates a cool effect and there is excellent application of straw, bamboo, and rattan to remind the tourist what kind of foreign land he is in. The immense boulders thrown up on the island by some prehistoric upheaval beneath the sea are used dramatically in the gardens that surround the hotel. Together with clusters of cactus and palms they give a feeling of being in another world.

CASA MONTEGO

Another Caribbean resort that succeeds in enchanting its guests is the 100-room Casa Montego in Jamaica (see illustrations, page 71). The eight-story hotel was designed by Ballard, Todd and Snibbe and the interiors by T. Eaton and Company of Toronto. It is a hotel that relies on the fair weather of the tropics. Though each room has an individual air-conditioner, great dependence is placed on the breeze that flows through the screen of native tile lining the corridors overlooking pool deck and terraces. The hotel is unusual in that there is little public space. There is a small lobby, plus a cardroom and bar on the ground floor, but the dining, lounging, and dancing take place on the pool deck and terraces cut into a heavily jungled cliff. The bar, a dark room with walls of native rock and mahogany paneling, is in sharp contrast with the open-air lounging areas. It is a hotel that could only work in the tropics and with a clientele not relying on the hotel management for entertainment around the clock.

The floors of the guestrooms are cement tile with rugs of grass fiber, so there is no worry on the part of guest or management about the effects of bathing suits and wet feet. Everything about the hotel, in fact, is designed for the casual vacationer; comfort is the goal, not opulence.

NASSAU BEACH LODGE

Proximity to Miami Beach seems to make it difficult for management to resist making a hotel overly-dramatic. There seems to be some fear that the hotel will not be able to compete. Take the case of the first Howard Johnson hotel built overseas. The Nassau Beach Lodge was designed by Charles McKirahan of Fort Lauderdale and the interiors were done by Contract Interiors. The job started off well with instructions from Howard Johnson to keep the place from being too jazzy. The aim was a West Indian atmosphere. Well and good. The hotel was cleanly done in a Scandinavian vein. Colors were muted in the large areas, accented only in the accessories and the plantings. There was a great deal of teak and rattan, all of it fitting nicely into the image that Nassau has projected in its extensive advertising programs in the United States. The bar serving the poolside lounge was thatched. Even in the lobby there were only simple groupings of furniture, much of it Danish. Just about the time *Interiors* magazine was writing of the tranquil sophistication of the Nassau Beach Lodge, somebody decided that it was not dramatic enough. The renovation was certainly no improvement, seeming to accent the negative.

BALMORAL HOTEL

The same thing happened at the Balmoral Hotel in Bal Harbour, next door to the Americana Hotel. The owners felt they needed to do something to make the older hotel more like its lively neighbor. So in came new lamps and draperies of a more lavish style. More often than not, such a frivolous approach to making over a hotel is a mistake.

The interiors of a resort hotel must be approached from the point of view of the potential guest. If the image of the hotel and its environment is one of placidity, nothing is to be gained by the introduction of noisy decoration.

III—RESORT HOTELS

Illustrations

The text for this Chapter will be found on pages 43 to 55

HOTEL EL CONVENTO, SAN JUAN, PUERTO RICO

Designer: Popi Alegria, A.I.D.

Photography: Alexandre Georges

Built more than three centuries ago, a former Carmelite convent is today one of the world's distinguished hotels. Dime store heir R. Frederick Woolworth found the former convent being used as a garage for garbage trucks and for slum housing. With the blessing of the church, he made a major investment in his belief that a different cultural environment would attract the well-heeled tourist. Detailed study for all phases of the restoration work was done by Ricardo Alegria, brother of the designer and head of the Institute of Puerto Rican culture. Furniture, carpets, fabrics, and tapestry for the lobby were made at the Fundacion Generallisimo Franco in Spain. Art objects came from antique shops in Madrid. Chairs beneath the tapestry are copies of those used in Spain 200 years ago.

Right. No two bedrooms are alike, this one has canopy beds which are copies of the Cardinal's bed at the Hostel de Reyes Catolicos. The fabric is a pattern of red and gray grape leaves. Light switches and door handles were brought in from Spain.

Below. Entrance to the hotel is on Cristo Street, a winding and twisting avenue paved with blue cobblestones brought to the island as ballast in Spanish merchant ships.

Facing page. Now the dining room seating 220, this was once the chapel. The walls are three feet thick and the small windows keep the room cool. Because acoustics was a problem in the 55-foot-high narrow room, tapestries, carpeting, and upholstered chairs were used to intercept sound bouncing from the stucco walls. The mural over the balcony was painted by Rafael Seco in Spain and installed in strips.

58

It was Olé and cha-cha-cha and just about everything else in the overdoing of the Seville lobby. The attempt at lavishness for the 300-room hotel produced an over-large lobby with little to make a guest at ease. The great curving glass mural on the front desk wall was done by Paul Simone. Lobby is on two levels, but there is no separation of the great space.

SEVILLE HOTEL, MIAMI BEACH, FLA.

Architecture: Melvin Grossman
Interiors: Henry End Associates
Photography: Alexandre Georges

CARIBE HILTON, SAN JUAN, PUERTO RICO

Architecture: Toro & Ferrer
Interiors: Inge V. Beck
Photography: Miguel Angel

Below. The first grand hotel for tourists in the Caribbean, the Caribe Hilton proved you could please the traveling American without smothering him with pretentiousness. The proof is in the 100-room Garden Wing (at left) which had to be added. The two buildings are connected by a covered walkway that traverses a tropical garden with fountains and pools. Bordering the walk are shops stocked with island handcrafts.

Above. Strong architectural lines and simple building materials are softened throughout the hotel by plantings and such luxurious furnishings as this island-made rug with its free-flowing design in gold, brown, and orange.

LA CONCHA, SAN JUAN, PUERTO RICO

Architecture: Toro & Ferrer; Warner, Burns,
Toan & Lunde, Associates
Interiors: Carson, Pirie, Scott & Co.
Photography: Alexandre Georges

Below. The 12-story main body of this hotel contains the guest suites. It is parallel to the ocean and protects the pool terrace behind it from the prevailing trade winds. The low lobby lies between the cabañas in the foreground (which are designed as living quarters for guests) and the guest wing which is thus set far back from traffic noises.

Above. Water garden in the lobby is open to the sky and features a sand cast sculpture by Nocito and Bert Schwartz. Looking up through the garden, one sees the terrace and guest wing. With a benevolent nature that could be trusted year round, the architects had no need to envelop the guests with lobby walls and draperies.

HAVANA RIVIERA, HAVANA, CUBA

Architecture: Polevitzky-Johnson Associates
Interiors: Albert Parvin
Photography: Alexandre Georges, guestroom,
               Rudi Rada

Above. The Riviera was the first American-sponsored hotel in Havana frankly designed to attract the gambling-minded tourist from Miami Beach. Anywhere one walked in the low-ceilinged sumptuous lobby, there was the merry mixture of sounds from the casino with its slot machines whirring and ivory dice clicking, plus the Latin tempo of the music from the cocktail lounge. Beyond the gossamer curtains were the pool deck and cabañas.

Left. Luxury of the public rooms continued into the guest rooms of the Riviera where color schemes were co-related with case goods, carpeting, lamps, and draperies which were handscreened so that patterns came out even at the floor and ceiling.

Above left. Fidel Castro changed the name to the Habana Libre, but he could do nothing to remove from the 30-story building an aura that was created by the forces of free enterprise. The eye level here is at the second-floor pool terrace ringed with cabañas. The block-square ground level is a labyrinth of shops, gardens, and ramps for automobile traffic.

Above right. Modern day version of the atrium is this garden courtyard under a concrete dome studded with plastic skylights. It provided an exotic first impression for guests entering from the street. Fully grown trees reach to the second floor which contained the social life of the hotel with ballrooms, casino, restaurants, and cocktail lounge.

Right. Luxury abounded in the suites on the upper floors of the hotel. In the Caribe suite, the floor of marble was graced with a hand woven rug inspired by a painting by Servando Cabrera Moreno. From the corner balcony one could view the heart of Havana and the historic Morro Castle.

HABANA HILTON, HAVANA CUBA

Architecture and Interiors: Welton Becket and
                               Associates
Photography: Lionel Freedman

FONTAINEBLEAU HOTEL, MIAMI BEACH, FLA.

Architecture and Interiors: Morris Lapidus Associates

Above. The 440-foot arc of the original guest wing faces the prevailing southwest breeze, overlooking the extensive pool and cabaña area and the formal gardens (foreground). Total area is eight and a half acres.

Below. The garden lobby is one step down from the main level. Five plastic bubbles light the pool at its center.

EDEN ROC HOTEL, MIAMI BEACH, FLA.

Architecture and Interiors: Morris Lapidus
Associates

Photography: Ezra Stoller

Above. Spectacular staircase is a lobby signature for the architect. Several types of marble were used here with Fulget tiles around the base of the stairs and a balustrade in the shape of brass urns. To the rear center in this picture white shades provide the background for lobby furniture upholstered in blues and purples. Carpet is gold.

Right. The Eden Roc stands 14 stories high between the ocean and Indian Creek waterway.

AMERICANA HOTEL, BAL HARBOUR, FLA.

Architecture and Interiors: Morris Lapidus
Associates
Photography: Ezra Stoller

Above. Sump brick is used for one wall of the lanai suites that overlook the pool terrace. Colors are keyed to either a tangerine or an aquamarine strip in the carpet.

Left. Architect Lapidus is especially good in the design of hotel bathrooms. This area includes a dressing room, twin lavatory with sliding plastic screen separating toilet and tub.

Below, left. Terra cotta tile is used for balcony grilles in an irregular pattern across the south wall of the 14-story guest wing.

ARUBA CARIBBEAN, WILLEMSTAD, NETHERLANDS ANTILLES

Architecture and Interiors: Morris Lapidus
Associates

Photography: Gelberg-Victor

Left. Perched on stilts to catch the breeze are the 140 guest rooms of the hotel. The gardens and terraces are built out to the sea and framed with grotesque boulders and giant cacti native to the island.

Facing page. The cement floor and the mosaic columns in the lobby create a cool atmosphere. Furnishings have simple lines and there is no attempt to overpower the vacationer.

Below. In the coffee shop, as elsewhere in the public spaces, we see the use of materials native to the island. Chairs are wicker and wrought iron. Tables are topped with mica. The wall is of native stone and the floor is cement tile. Over the counter is a wood frame spaced with plastic light diffusers.

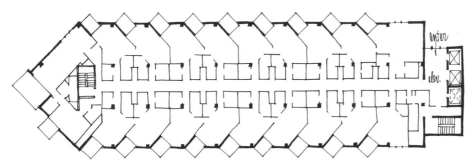

Above. With the main wing of the hotel at right angles to the ocean, the architect angled the rooms 30 percent to afford all guests a view of the sea. This view of the courtyard is from the two-story guest wing that completes the hotel's U-shaped plan.

Below. Scandinavian styled furnishings in the guest rooms suit the casual atmosphere of the island resort. Connecting doors and convertible sofas provide great flexibility of accommodations. Tops of tables and casegoods are in teak-patterned plastic.

NASSAU BEACH LODGE, NASSAU, BAHAMAS

Architecture: Charles McKirahan
Interiors: Contract Interiors
Photography: Louis Reens

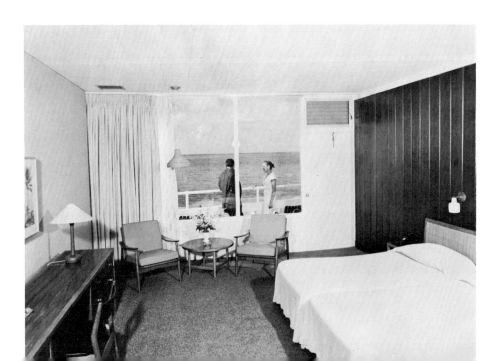

CASA MONTEGO, JAMAICA

Architecture: Ballard, Todd & Snibbe
Interiors: T. Eaton and Company
Photography: Alexandre Georges

Above. Open-air lobby is beneath the central hotel building. The patterned far wall is native cement tile in blues and white. Floor is gray and white terrazzo.

Below. All guest rooms are the same size and are furnished alike though in two different arrangements. In layout shown here in which beds are cornered, the combination luggage storage and headboard is cut away to save one foot of floor area per room. Designed to suit the casual resort atmosphere of Jamaica, guest roms have walls of rough white plaster and the floors are cement tile covered with grass rugs. Paneling of African Limba plywood encloses one of the two capacious closets provided on either side of the bathroom door. The drawer-cupboard unit (like desk and side tables not shown) is framed in black metal with panels of yellow and white. In duty-free Jamaica, it was possible to import the rattan chairs from Hong Kong, the armchairs from Italy, the casegoods and beds from Canada, and rugs from Japan.

CARLTON BEACH HOTEL
HAMILTON, BERMUDA

Architecture: William Tabler
Interiors: Henry End Associates
Photography: Ezra Stoller

Above. While colors in the lobby and dining rooms are brilliantly tropical, in the guest rooms the tones are muted. Each of the 200 rooms in the hotel has a six-foot-deep balcony running the full width of the room.

Facing page. Lobby floor and the cantilevered staircase are white terrazzo. Cushions on the reed benches are a colorful stripe and the seating area over on the right is defined by a rug of multicolored squares in different depths of pile; against its off-white background are tropical colors of tangerine, pink, and fuschia.

Left. Beyond these swinging doors attached to the screen of bleached cypress is the Southampton cocktail lounge.

CANEEL BAY PLANTATION, ST. JOHN, VIRGIN ISLANDS

Architecture: LaFarge, Knox & Murphy
Interiors: Ann Hatfield Associates
Photography: exterior, Alexandre Georges,
                Ron Morrisette

Everything at Caneel Bay was keyed to the serenity of the island. Furnishings were designed for guests who came to relax, not to see or be seen and most of them are from Denmark, once the mother country of the Virgin Islands. The designer used natural colors of stone and wood and kept the interiors simple. Walls of native stone and masonry divide the row of guest accommodations, each with its own private patio overlooking the beach. Drawn up into a neat band across the glass wall is a woven wood blind. The rug is Haitian sisal.

Right. Waterside view showing steps leading down to beach from the individual patios.

HILTON HAWAIIAN VILLAGE, HONOLULU, HAWAII

Architecture and Interiors: Welton Becket and
Associates

Photography: Werner Stoy and R. Wenkham

Henry Kaiser's original idea for the Hawaiian Village was a group of low buildings scattered about the beach.

Left. The two-story section contains only guest rooms whose occupants have the advantage of a pool right on their doorstep. Every room has a balcony with shoji screens providing privacy from the neighbors.

Below. In this three-story section of the hotel, the ground floor is one continuous open space; the two top stories of guest rooms have the same balcony arrangements as above.

Top left. Exotic colors of the island are contrasted with the lava rock wall in this lobby area. The bamboo is an inexpensive screen for utility pipes in the ceiling. Kappa shell serves as diffuser for the lighting in the columns. The convoluted pottery lamps stand on tables of koa wood. Flooring is vinyl tile.

Left. The Makahiki is the newest—and most luxurious—of the hotel's dining rooms with a full gourmet menu. The tropical theme is carried out with bamboo light shades containing exotic plantings, and painted ceiling.

IV—INTERNATIONAL HOTELS

The 20th century jet traveler can circle the globe and stay each night in hotels that strike the same note of style and comfort.

This is not the result of any lack of imagination on the part of the world's new innkeepers, but is simply a case of supplying a demand. The sophisticated traveler — movie star, oil executive, government official, or well-heeled tourist — expects to find a familiar degree of luxury in a hotel whether it be in New York, Athens, Tel Aviv, or Bangkok.

He will certainly look for local color, but this is something he prefers to see from the balcony of his air-conditioned bedroom or through an expanse of glass as he sips a very cold martini and tests the rareness of his sirloin or prime rib. He will enjoy walking through a lobby that provides a look at the native arts of a strange land, but the craftsmanship will go for naught if the beds are uncomfortable and the hot water pipes are not constantly filled.

It is not necessarily a good thing, but modern techniques of construction and interior design have provided an international style for hotels that is the same on the banks of the Nile as it is in a grand motel at the mouth of a turnpike in Oklahoma City. But in both places there must be an incorporation of local color that gives a hotel a distinct personality and warmth and makes it different from the stopover last night and the one of tomorrow.

The unique skills and experience of the American hotel industry have inherent in them a trap of which the architect and designer must be aware. It is the danger of exporting the know-how without taking into account and using the distinctive personality of the particular place in a blend that will satisfy the customers for those new bedrooms and public spaces.

Emmanuel Gran, Director of Architecture and Interior Design for Hilton Hotels International, has said many times that whenever possible he tries to use architects, designers, and artists of the country in which a hotel is being constructed. This is an admirable statement, but a debatable point of view. Certainly, it is understandable that local architects should be called on for their knowledge of native materials, codes, and idiosyncracies within the local building trades. But the most successful international hotels are those that have had the benefit of American experience. Despite the psychological and political advantages of bringing in native architects and designers, there is the practical factor of experience to be taken into account, and it is possible that the real aim of the Hilton design department is to keep strong control over foreign projects by employing people with little or no experience in hotel work.

The average architect in foreign lands does not have hotel experience. If he has any background in this field, it was probably gained before World War II and therefore is based on early European ideas. This was the type of background that produced the early hotels in the United States and is now considered hopelessly obsolete.

Is this to say that hotels everywhere in the world must depend on American architects and interior designers? Not exactly. But they must have the benefit of contemporary hotel experience that is, at the moment, practically an American monopoly.

NILE HILTON

The Nile Hilton (see illustrations, page 93) is an excellent example of the combination of this experience with the skills of native artisans. Representing a total design concept of Welton Becket & Associates of Los Angeles, the Nile Hilton was certainly not built for Egyptians, yet it incorporates the finest of Middle Eastern craftsmanship and provides the special kind of romance that the world traveler seeks. Before the design work ever got underway, Becket talked with Egyptian officials about organizing the arts of the country. His design team quickly discovered the excellent woodworkers, the spinners and weavers, the metal workers skilled in the handling of brass that were available in Egypt. Egyptian museums and historical shrines yielded source material for design concepts. Furniture styling was derived from ancient prototypes. The ballroom mural in Venetian glass mosaic was inspired by tomb paintings at Thebes. The same type of mosaic was used for the streetside facade of the 12-story, 400-room hotel. The mural, measuring 25 by 280 feet, incorporates Egyptian hieroglyphs and would fit into the rarified atmosphere of New York's Museum of Modern Art. Huge lamps of pierced brass hang above cantilevered staircases; here again is a successful marriage of ancient arts with modern building techniques.

The main dining room, called Jewel of the Nile, overlooks the historic river. There are expanses of draperies, across which cruise sailboats that Cleopatra found perfect for dalliance with visiting Romans. The material is natural linen and the boats are grey and blue; not printed, but appliqued with a stitch the nomadic Bedouin uses to decorate the inside of his tent.

Throughout the hotel is a myriad of such examples of ancient symbolism adapted to a contemporary manner. In the guestrooms are many decorative items inspired by those preliminary visits to the museums. There are handwoven draperies printed with a lotus design taken from Thebes and a tile motif for the rug from the same source. Bas relief, cast from originals in the Cairo museum, is used to adorn the walls. Coffee tables are graced with aprons of Mashrabieh grille-work. There is liberal use of brass lamps and brass tray tables in the guest suites.

The Becket designers were astounded by the skill of Egyptian plasterers and made excellent use of their talents in the ceilings of public areas. In the bar, panels made of colored bits of blown glass fashion birds glow from backlighting that is natural by day and man-made by night.

In her comprehensive review of the Nile Hilton in *Interiors* Editor, Olga Gueft, wrote:

> The total effect is not of a pastiche, but of a unique place with a
> palpable soul. Magnificence has a tendency to be a bit crushing,
> but here the expanses of smooth white marble and fresh, soft,
> sunny pastels give the spectator no burden, but a lift. This is a

triumph, and so is the peculiarly intuitive imagination and sensitive skill in deploying the amazing riches that dazzle the spirit in this fairyland interior.

With all respect to designers and craftsmen of every land, successful jobs like the Nile Hilton lend weight to the theory that an outsider usually has a better idea of what constitutes good local color than does the local designer. The stranger, if he has the taste and experience, can do a better job of creating within a hotel a feeling that is indigenous to the country. He will avoid cluttering up the place with too many examples of local color. As a stranger, he will be more impersonal and therefore more selective. An analogy can be found in the movie industry, for it is in Hollywood that, from a stage set point of view, some of the best films of British life have been made.

Then one might ask, would a French or British designer be able to do a better job on a new hotel in Milwaukee than the native of Wisconsin? He very well might if he had the requisite amount of modern hotel experience. Throughout the world there are examples of successful hotels that represent the finest of team efforts by wise management and experienced architects and designers. With such a combination, there is no limit to what can be achieved.

ROYAL HOTEL, COPENHAGEN

But immediately, of course, there comes to mind the most dramatic exception to this rule. For in Copenhagen stands the Royal Hotel of the Scandinavian Airlines System and it represents the genius of one man, Professor Arne Jacobsen. If he had previously created a grand hotel, then it is a secret from the world. In the 22-story Royal, Jacobsen has created a monument not to himself, but to the highest ideals of man's creativity. When the pretentious palaces of Miami Beach, Hawaii, and Las Vegas are washed away by a future tidal wave of good taste, the Royal will be looked to as a guidepost and a beacon of timeless elegance. Of this hotel the British publication, *Interior Design* said,

> From any viewpoint, this is a building which, in the unity of its structure, form, furnishings and equipment, and in the perfection of its detailed design, proclaims vigorously the supremacy of the master-architect as a creator of human environment.

To which I can only add that if all architects were such creators of space, interior designers would have to close up shop and look for other work. Fortunately for the designer, most architects are so concerned with the creation of physical space that they never think of designing for people. It is their erector-set approach to interiors, so loudly applauded in the architectural trade journals, that brings management running to the designer in search of human warmth. Architects fall into the trap of creating such monumental spaces that the human element is trampled. This might be fine in the lobby of a bank when the purpose is to create respect for the institution, but in a hotel it can be disastrous. The guest is made to feel puny and insignificant in a building that should be cheering. (In passing, however, note should be taken of the trend toward more warmth through

We take the same line with our designers that we take with our chefs: we don't tell them how to cook, but what to cook.

Curt R. Strand, V.P.
Hilton International

The sterile and clinical aspect of architecture, or perhaps building would be a better reference, has supplied the impetus on the part of owners and management to engage the interior designer to supply an environment complementing the emotional requirements of the human beings who must occupy these engineered interior spaces.

Harry Anderson, Publisher
Interior Design

the use of art in the glass towers of Manhattan and other capitals of the world.)

Another chore that falls to the designer is the hiding of engineering and architectural mistakes. This is particularly true of mechanical equipment. If you doubt it, look up the next time you walk into a hotel lobby or banquet hall. Chances are the ceiling will make a great show of the mechanical guts of the building. A good interior designer, when brought into a project at its inception, can demonstrate his worth in sparing the guest this insight into the air-conditioning, lighting, or sound systems of the hotel.

A. Kappenberger, the Manager of the Royal in Copenhagen has acknowledged that many of the features incorporated in the hotel resulted from his visits to the United States. This does not, however, detract at all from architect Jacobsen's handling of the job. For it was his from the skin of the enameled panels to the faucets in the bathrooms.

It is not enough to produce dramatic schemes of exterior and internal spaces. The walls of architectural colleges are covered with solutions to design problems, each more exotic than the next. Concept is one thing, but it must always be carried out to the point of detailing if the project is to succeed. The Royal Hotel is an excellent example of a combination of the two (see illustrations, page 96).

The 20-story guestroom tower of this hotel rises from a base on four levels, two of which are above grade. The area used as the SAS air terminal is two floors in height and there are ground level shops with entrances both on the street and from the lobby. On the first lower level are the usual barbershop, public washrooms, and storage. Below this is a parking garage for 200 cars and mechanical shops for hotel maintenance crews.

Jacobsen's signatures in the interiors of the Royal are his famous Egg and Swan chairs and they are found from lobby to guestroom in varying dimensions. These will for a long time engender lively debate over form and function, but they do serve to set the hotel apart from the mainstream of international style which tends to sterility.

Another factor that sets this hotel apart is the lighting, all Jacobsen-designed. In an issue of the fine Dutch publication, *International Lighting Review,* there is critical comment concerning the low key of illumination in the guestrooms, considered by the editors to be insufficient for comfortable reading. However, there is nothing but praise for the architect's design and handling of lighting in the public areas, particularly in the dark-walled lobby. In it, incandescent reflector lamps are recessed in the ceiling, spilling a soft and even light. Of the Royal lobby, the Dutch journal commented,

> In this dark environment the lighting ornament above the reception counter draws the visitor as irresistibly as the moth is drawn
> to the flame. This ornament, a bright idea in itself, demonstrates
> the architect's endeavor and ability to create something handsome
> with quite simple means.

The band of light floods from behind squares of sheet metal sprayed white. The corridors in the hotel are short and the guest never has a fear of becoming lost in a maze. Above each door is a fluorescent tube shielded by a diffuser panel. It is a quieter version of the system used at the Orly

Airport Hotel in Paris where each doorway is marked by a luminous panel in the ceiling. These set up a pattern of stripes down the long corridor while in the Royal there is a more even effect with highlights at each room entrance.

Writing in the *International Lighting Review,* Jacobsen said this of his approach to the physical being of the Royal Hotel,

> On artistic grounds it was important to try and make as light a building as possible because of the great height and mass of the block which would very easily overpower the surrounding buildings and appear to give an unfortunate heaviness over the neighboring Tivoli Gardens. One grey-green sheet of glass divided up by anodized mullions in a unity without special architronic divisions was the only solution which I thought would give the least dominating sort of building.
>
> The glass color was selected with reference to the sky and the reflection of the clouds. A stronger colored glass would probably, under some conditions of light, seem gayer and more lively, but in another light the effect would have been too heavy and bombastic. The reflection of the weather gives the building a changing character which, I felt, was more important than striving for a stronger effect. The light, high blocks need a heavier base, which is why a darker, grey-green enamel cladding was chosen.

The greys and greens are carried inside. Spread over the lobby floor of light-grey marble are a half dozen shadings of grey and green in area rugs and upholstery. In the bedrooms, the colors move into neutrals, seeking a more common denominator of personal taste.

THE ENGLISH HOTEL SCENE

Arne Jacobsen deserves homage but it must again be stressed that he is an exceptional man and that the most successful hotels built in the world have been by those with a background within the industry. In a special issue on hotels in 1958 an editor of the British magazine, *Design,* wrote that hotel operators in England

> seem reluctant to acknowledge modern developments towards higher standards of comfort, durability and ease of maintenance in the design of furnishings and fittings and seem content to depend on eclectic traditional designs. . . . The widespread acceptance of modern interiors, particularly in America and on the Continent, will lead visitors to expect a hotel environment that will at least be as comfortable and pleasing as they are at home.

The writer predicted public areas would become less elaborate and less important; that bedrooms would be smaller, yet better planned and furnished.

In preparation for the special issue, the editors had invited leaders of Britain's hotel industry to participate in a panel discussion. Some of the comments made then bear repeating. They indicate how a guarding of tradition kept Britain's hotel industry from playing its proper role in the international scheme of jet travel. Because British hotel men were not progressive, they invited an American invasion. It was of this that the editors of *Design* were trying to give warning in 1958.

Forecasting a 400 per cent increase in trans-Atlantic air travel by 1963, the magazine pointed out that the postwar record of hotel construction in Great Britain was a sad one. It was even necessary to remark that the visitor from America would expect to find a bathroom in his room and that few British hotels could provide it. As for interior design, the editor wrote,

> The large quantity of new home building since the war, and the growing acceptance of good modern furniture, have resulted in standards of design and amenity far beyond those normally to be found in medium and small hotels.

This chapter is not intended as a flogging place for my former country-men, England just happens to be a country I know well. But I must quote one remark made at that hotel conference by Captain K. C. McCallum, managing director of Trust Houses Ltd., who represented the British Hotels and Restaurant Association. After he had gloomily predicted a worldwide recession, Captain McCallum was asked why at least four American cor-porations were struggling with the problem of finding locations for new hotels in London. "Wait until they burn their fingers," the Captain said. The subsequent American successes must have been unnerving. Though all at the conference seemed agreed that London did not have sufficient hotels to take care of the tourists from America, there was doubt that the industry could afford to put up new buildings. An emphatic "No" came from Group Captain B. G. Carfoot, a Director of Ind Coope & Allsop, who represented the viewpoint of brewer-management of commercial hotels. He explained that his company was not too concerned with tourist business, but did try to exploit it during the summer months. "I do not think that today new hotels can ever be built to give anything like a reasonable return just for the tourist trade alone," he said. But the Captain acknowledged that his observations of the American tourist led him to believe they expected more luxurious accommodations and a higher standard of service that the British hotels were providing.

In that same year in America, Sheraton President, Ernest Henderson, was saying, "We have become more and more convinced that in these com-petitive times the best in hotel services often can best be achieved only through new construction."

CARLTON TOWER

When the Hotel Corporation of America made its decision to join in the construction of the Carlton Tower in London in 1960, President A. M. Sonnabend recognized all the risk involved in public relations. Several years earlier, Knott Hotels had opened the Westbury, a semi-commercial hotel designed by Michael Rosenauer, Fellow of the Royal Institute of British Architects and also a Member of the American Institute of Archi-tects. In the Westbury, the interiors were handled by couturieres. The ap-pointments may have been suited to the queen, but they were out of place in a contemporary hotel.

The same architect was commissioned by Sir Robert McAlpine and

Sons, the British investors who put up the Carlton Tower, but Hotel Corporation of America called on our offices for the interiors. The job represented a great challenge because I was, in a sense, going home again. And there was some understandable resentment and an attitude of "show us". Just as soon as the Carlton Tower was announced in the press, there were outcries. Letters to *The Times* of London protested against "shiny skyscraper type of American hotels" going up in what was considered an elegant residential neighborhood. It was not really a skyscraper, but an 8-story building combined with a 16-story tower. The job became a matter of beating the British at their own game, of making the Carlton less opulent and more understated than the British would have done themselves. Londoners were convinced they wouldn't like it even before the walls went up.

With all of this as a prelude, it was gratifying when a year later England's *Interior Design* magazine said:

> the scheme has been carried out with a commendable lack of vulgarity or ostentation — particularly when one considers that the hotel caters in its 318 rooms for the luxury tourist and the expense-account executive.

I did not escape whole, however. The writer prefaced these remarks with the reminder to his readers that the interiors had been done within the limitations of an admittedly theatrical technique, referring to my background as a designer of movie sets in Hollywood immediately upon my post-war departure from England.

The magazine, in common with design magazines everywhere, had fault to find with the building, calling it an ill-proportioned facade with tiers of "clumsily detailed balconies making confusion worse confounded." Whether as a compliment or a rebuke I do not know, he wrote that on crossing the threshold,

> one enters a totally different world, for unlike that other American-operated London hotel (the Westbury), the Carlton Tower has an interior designed in the style most commonly found in new hotels in America itself. The ingredients of this style, familiar to most British people through the media of the films and the glossy magazines, include decorations with white and gold, a mixture of modern furniture and upholstered pieces and accessories with a distinctly traditional flavor, and the introduction, as an important element of the decor, of outsize table lamps which, in bedrooms and sitting rooms, provide the sole source of artificial lighting.

American journalists may argue with the syntax and the length of the sentence, but I will take it as a compliment to myself and to the design profession in America.

In designing the Carlton Tower, caution was needed against the trap of trying to copy British period design, something the British themselves are best at. The greatest furniture craftsmen have been English — Chippendale, Adams, Hepplewhite. To have copied them would have been a terrible mistake; to have tried a fake period design in a country steeped in tradition would have been folly. I recall that management felt the Rib Room of the

The so-called clean contemporary furniture has met with a rather cold reception from hotel guests. This contemporary or international style does not seem to create an air of excitement and luxury.

Morris Lapidus, Architect

Carlton Tower should be an imitation of an English inn or tavern. I thought that nothing could be worse and I argued for a more contemporary look since it would have been laughable to produce an imitation tavern in a country where there are so many authentic ones.

A real effort was made to avoid the use of synthetics in the hotel, relying instead on natural materials turned out by British craftsmen. Even before the hotel got under way, there were stories that all the furnishings would be imported from America. This was not true. Except for the stacking chairs used in the banquet room and some of the upholstered pieces in the suites, most of the furnishings came from the British Isles. In some cases, materials were imported and crafted according to designs by our office. There were rosewoods from Bombay, silks from Italy and Thailand. The carpeting was woven in Britain. The mural in the lobby executed in glass was by Felix Topolski. This famous Londoner is a Pole. He also did much of the wall decoration in the public rooms of the Carlton Tower. For the Rib Room, where typically English oak is used for paneling, Topolski did vignettes of contemporary British life. They are full of whimsy, much in the manner of the Hirshfeld drawings featured in the theater section of the Sunday *New York Times*.

Because I often run into this question of hands-across-the-sea design, I like to tell a story from an international exhibition held in Denmark. Three countries were asked to pick the best representatives of their art. Britain sent Topolski, a Pole. France sent Marcel Vertes, a Hungarian. America sent Saul Steinberg, a Roumanian.

The art work by Topolski with its genuine flavor of British life, helps greatly in keeping the Carlton Tower from presenting such an international picture that the guest might forget he is in England. It is certainly a preferable method to that of copying styles from Ye Olde Blue Boar Inn. All of the furnishings in the hotel were designed to give a contemporary feeling which would not fall completely in the international idiom. They were also designed to be sumptuous without violating the British desire for understatement.

The air conditioned hotel offers a wide variety of accommodations. There are 66 possible combinations of suites with two, three, and four rooms; 133 rooms with twin beds, 29 with double beds, and 37 with living rooms. Of course, every room has its own bath with shower, automatic dialing for hotel service, radio, and television.

RITZ IN LISBON

The grand hotel, while it may have been a product of young America, is not thought of in European terms. The new Ritz in Lisbon is considered to be one of the most luxurious and expensive hotels built in recent times (see illustrations, page 102). Everything about it smells of money, lots of it. The Ritz is typically European, with a classicism and heaviness, from the wedding cake approach of the ten-story tower to the ponderous furniture in the lobby. The furnishings are neither period nor modern and can only be described as being opposed to the modern Scandinavian approach. Geared to luxury service, the Ritz has a staff of 500 for its 300 rooms, a proportion that far exceeds the one-to-one ratio found in most modern hotels.

It is in its art work that the Ritz makes its best mark. The finest of national talent was enlisted to produce the tapestries, the sculpture, and the murals. All of these are striking, but in the guestrooms, design rolls backward to a bygone day. Furnishings are stiff and inadequate. In one bedroom can be seen a small dressing table that is not suitable for the 20th century traveler with her paraphernalia of beauty aids. Canopy beds are romantic and can be used in a hotel that is attempting to create old world atmosphere. However, the Ritz is a new hotel in a cosmopolitan city. It was designed according to the dictates of modern architecture. The use of tester beds in what has been called the most imposing new hotel building in Europe must certainly be considered pretentious. At best, they are dust catchers. The answer that help is inexpensive and that the designer was thus free from worry over problems of maintenance is inadequate.

KARACHI INTERCONTINENTAL

New York architect William Tabler, a man who had 200 million dollars worth of hotel projects on his drawing board one year, has often been criticized for designing an American-type hotel abroad. In a study of the architect's role in hotel design, *Architectural Record* examined the criticism directed at Tabler for his Karachi Intercontinental, a seven million dollar project for the hotel subsidiary of Pan American World Airways. Tabler had been taken to task for his unrelenting efforts to design for fewer and fewer employees. Why bother, said the critics, when hotel help in Pakistan is available at a fraction of western standards. The magazine pointed out that Tabler always recognizes the architect's responsibility for tomorrow's operation. He believes it his duty to design for the day when in countries like Pakistan pay scales will become as big a budget headache as they are in New York, London, and Paris.

In the scheme for the hotel Karachi, Tabler provided the same versatility of space as he did in the Statler in Dallas or the Hilton in Pittsburgh. Public areas were kept small and the ballroom was designed to accommodate any size of group and to be closed off completely in the off-season.

Tabler's attitude toward hotel design is a basic one.

They are by definition products of travel, and today there are
more travelers flying from one destination to another in less than
a day. We must provide rooms for them.

The man who has supplied more of those rooms than anyone else is, of course, Conrad Hilton. His name is synonymous with the travel revolution that took place after World War II. It was a revolution tied closely to the outburst of nationalism that created dozens of new nations, all of them seeking status. The international hotel quickly became a symbol of progress. And Hilton was the magic name and the catalyst between bubbling nationalism and American hotel experience.

In his autobiography, *Be My Guest,* Hilton tells of the postwar suggestions by American government officials that the Hilton organization be used as an instrument in the foreign aid programs. The Departments of State and Commerce were interested in stimulating trade and travel through

He does not want a home from home . . . hotel interiors are on the threshold of show business. The visitor arriving from Detroit does not want to find his new hotel identical with his last 6,000 miles away.

*Stephen Garrett
Design*

the establishment of American-operated hotels in key cities of the world. The aim was to inject American dollars into war-torn economics of our friends overseas. The hotel program offered an alternative to a simple handout. We have seen how this worked first in Puerto Rico. The story was repeated in Turkey, a country seeking to throw off the stigma of being called "the sick man of Europe." The Turkish government put up seven million dollars to build a 300-room hotel and Hilton supplied the planning. This included the training in the United States of a score of Turks for key positions. The lease guaranteed Hilton one-third of the gross profit.

THE ISTANBUL HILTON

The Istanbul Hilton (see illustrations, page 104) was successful from the start. Designed by Skidmore, Owings and Merrill, it brought the cellular style of architecture to an ancient land. Except for a curved golden canopy, the lines are simple and crisp. From the honeycomb of balconies, the guests look across the mosques of Moslem to the Bosphorus. There are exotic touches throughout the hotel: a glass sheltered roof garden, a ladies' sitting room that is right out of the *Arabian Nights*, and balcony grilles of teak. But in the main the hotel presents a style that carries no national label. In its first year of operation, the hotel ran at ninety per cent occupancy and more than half the guests were Americans. These are the travelers who appreciate imaginative interiors in a hotel, but look first for the familiar comforts of home.

All hotels should represent a combination of escape, adventure, and even nostalgia. But the great danger lies in taking the interiors to a point of being bizarre. The Istanbul Hilton provides a fine example of modern building techniques softened by interiors that have a human approach. The modular atmosphere is eased by the use of local color, by reflecting pools, and by features like the blue tile roof of the supper club.

Conrad Hilton is as great a showman as he is a hotel man and the opening of a hotel overseas is the occasion of an international gala. When the Castellana Hilton was opened in Madrid in 1953, Hilton provided two plane loads of movie stars and café society to enchant his Spanish associates. There was only one trouble. The switchboard of the hotel was jammed for the first four days because so many Spanish ladies wanted to say hello to Gary Cooper. The entertainment was fabulous. It could hardly miss with a combination of Spanish gypsies and the singing of Mary Martin.

The story was repeated two years later in Turkey. The opening day guests included Sonja Henie, Carol Channing, Irene Dunne, and Merle Oberon. To make sure there would be first rate press coverage of the event, Hilton brought along Bob Considine, Hedda Hopper, and Louella Parsons.

In his autobiography, Hilton recalls the speech he made at the dedication of the hotel in Istanbul. "Each of our hotels is a little America, not as a symbol of bristling power, but as a friendly center where men of many nations and of good will may speak the language of peace," he said. This mingling of nations also added up to a dollar-green investment. In the first year, the hotel had a gross operating profit of $1,629,000. The hotel played a major part in the sixty per cent increase in tourism the country enjoyed.

Successfully established, the Hilton formula was used in a quick suc-

People may travel seeking a change from home, but they want homelike comforts and the personal concern of the management that they enjoy at home.

Paul Friedlander
Travel Editor
New York Times

cession of great cities of the world: Havana, West Berlin, Montreal, and Cairo. Then came the planning for Trinidad, London, Amsterdam, Rome, and Bangkok.

Speaking to the Commonwealth Club of San Francisco, Hilton had this to say about the hotel man as an international statesman:

> The operation of Hilton Hotels International has evolved from a unique philosophy. Rather than assume the role of invaders intent upon siphoning back all profits to the United States, we have joined hands in a business fellowship with foreign entrepreneurs. We operate hotels abroad for the same reason we operate them in this country — to make money for our stockholders. That is a fact for which we need not apologize. Indeed, it is a prime motivating force in this as in any other free economy. But if money were all we were after, we could make it right here in this country with a few less headaches.
>
> However, we feel that if we really believe in what we are saying about liberty, about communism, about happiness, that we as a nation must exercise our great strength and power for good against evil.
>
> If we really believe this, it is up to each of us, our organization and our industries, to contribute to this objective with all the resources at our command.

STOCKHOLM'S FORESTA HOTEL

One of the other important exports in the hotel industry has been Scandinavian design. This has become as much a part of international innkeeping as has America's cubicle, erector-set style of architecture. A fine example of Scandinavian design can be found on its home ground, in Stockholm's Foresta Hotel. Once a complete fake of a castle built around 1900 by an eccentric lady, the Foresta now comes close to providing hotel services like those of Dallas or New York. The original building was converted to hold a bar, restaurant, clubrooms, and a cafeteria with a terrace. Then came a group of five connected buildings, each of two stories with two and three room apartments for permanent guests and large families on tour. Then a 90-room standard hotel building was added with space for the necessary shops. To attract business groups during the tourist-less, cold winters, the Foresta owners built a convention hall seating 400, and also equipped to serve as a night club in the busy summer season.

Throughout the hotel, from the cherry paneling in the boutique shop to the chalked oak in the guestrooms, the Foresta represents artful work with good material, well executed and with excellent graphics. It embodies the understated good taste one has come to expect from Scandinavia.

ACCADIA GRAND HOTEL

One finds this same feeling in the Accadia Grand Hotel in Israel. In its excellent presentation of the hotel, *Interiors* magazine made the point that,

> In keeping with Israel's status as a pioneer nation, the Accadia avoids the super-glut striven for by the designers of the Florida

and Riviera hostelries. Generosity in the allotment of space, deft lighting, a play of raw materials (brick, exposed ceiling planks and beams) against finished ones, tapestries and other handwoven textiles of Accadian inspiration contribute to the Israeli atmosphere.

This 102-suite hotel on the shore of the Mediterranean was developed by South American investors. It attracts predominantly Latin American tourists, but the hotel's excellent facilities for banquets and meetings also draw business from nearby Tel Aviv, as does the cafeteria which is set on a terrace overlooking the sea.

The interiors were designed by Yeheskiel and Dvorah Gad who were trained as architects in Vienna. They had previously done the interiors of homes for several Israel governmental leaders and for several of the country's embassies abroad.

SHERATON TEL AVIV

While the Accadia is an example of local designers achieving a fine effect, the Sheraton hotel in Tel Aviv (see illustrations, page 109) demonstrates things that can go wrong under the same arrangement. With no control from headquarters in New York, local designers who obviously had little experience made an attempt to copy the Scandinavian look. The imitation is a poor one and Sheraton would have done better to import the real thing. It was the first Sheraton hotel built outside the United States and has 200 rooms with a ballroom that can seat 800. Its one saving grace is a sculpture wall created by Nehemiah Azaz. The Israeli artist used plaster blocks coated with cement to tell the story of the six civilizations that were buried by time and sand on the eastern shore of the Mediterranean.

The grandeur of this art is in sharp contrast with the interiors of the guestrooms. Some of them are frankly laughable. In one room, at least, is a lamp hung directly over the pillow of the bed because there was not enough space for a night table and a lamp. Happily, the light globe is made of plastic, not glass, so the damage might not be severe on sitting up suddenly during the night to answer the telephone. This is typical of hotels designed by those with little or no hotel experience.

THE ARIEL

Though it created quite a stir as the first circular hotel built in Europe, the Ariel near the London airport has interiors that reflect this same lack of experience. It is a four-story building with 186 rooms on the upper three floors. The circle is 176 feet in diameter and 48 feet high. The hole in the doughnut is a garden.

The Ariel was built by a group that included J. Lyons and Co., the largest restaurant operators in the world. The firm had previous hotel experience, but mainly with older hotels like the Regent Palace and the Cumberland in London. Probably because of the problems of operating these older places, the Ariel incorporates many automated features. There are radio communication systems for the staff and an electric letter rack that tells the guest if he has mail or a telephone message. Because of the proximity to the airport, double windows were installed and the flooring includes a layer of fiberglass.

EL SALVADOR

I am a great admirer of William Tabler's talents as an architect. One excellent example of his work is the El Salvador which he designed for the Intercontinental Hotel Corporation. The design follows the pattern of international style now so familiar: low-lying public areas from which rises the bedroom tower complete with balconies. Native materials are used extensively, but somehow what is created in the interiors is devoid of local color. One could easily imagine himself to be in Poughkeepsie, N. Y. As was pointed out in the case of the Foresta Hotel in Stockholm, there is great charm in understatement, but when this lacks style, the results are disappointing. In the El Salvador, the interior designer made an attempt at architectural clarity in the cocktail lounge. What he achieved, however, was a plainness that is positively painful.

EL PANAMA

A better pattern for interiors of such a tropical hotel was set by Florence Hayward at El Panama in Panama City. This was Edward Stone's pioneering effort in the establishment of the egg-crate facade that is now the trademark of the international hotel. It is a style that was incorporated very successfully in the public areas of the Caribe Hilton: low-scaled terraces open to trade winds that make air-conditioning unnecessary most of the time.

It is interesting, however, to check back on Stone and let him second-guess himself on the Panama job. *Architectural Forum* asked him what changes he would have made if he were doing the hotel over again. His answers are reflected in hotels subsequently done by other architects in other lands. Stone said he would not have put the public rooms on the first floor and rooftop of the main building. At El Panama, there were too many complaints about party noises from guests who had had a busy day with business or on tours and wanted only to get to sleep early. His alternative was a concentration of the guestrooms in a tower and a separation of restaurants, night clubs, and cocktail lounges at one end of the main building. We have seen this done in Tabler's El Salvador and a score of tropical resorts. Stone also suggested placing the lobby and elevators, plus kitchen and storage areas, at the point where public areas merge into the bedroom tower to provide more efficient hotel service and increase the sound barrier.

Stone would have revised his facade so that floor slabs halted at the balcony rail, eliminating the uneasiness of guests that some drunk or maniac might try fly-walking between rooms. Instead of double doors leading to the balcony, Stone felt greater advantage of the natural air-conditioning of the tradewinds could be taken with the use of sliding glass doors.

The hotels that followed in the next decade, notably Welton Becket's Habana Hilton, certainly bore out the value of Stone's hard second look at himself.

IV—INTERNATIONAL HOTELS

Illustrations

The text for this Chapter will be found on pages 79 to 91

NILE HILTON, CAIRO, EGYPT

Architecture and Interiors: Welton Becket
Associates

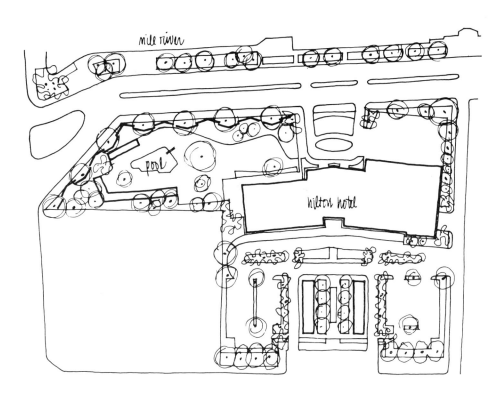

The Nile Hilton is built on a 6½-acre site at the Kasr El Nil Bridge in Cairo. The east facade is faced with Venetian glass mosaic of hieroglyphs transformed into a modern abstract. Measuring 25 feet x 180 feet, it is the world's largest glass mosaic. The second floor of the hotel extends on columns across the entrance driveway and serves to protect the lobby, walks, and shops beneath it. Many of the hotel's public rooms are on the second level.

NILE HILTON

Above. Marble walls and floor of the ballroom lounge reflect the vivid gold of the furniture upholstery and the yellow of the textured plaster ceiling. Panels of Mashrabieh doweling can be extended across the room to divide it for smaller functions. Styling of the chairs and tables was taken from old Egyptian prototypes. On the wall at left is a Venetian glass mural copied from tomb paintings at Thebes.

Top, facing page. Huge jeweled lamp of pierced brass hangs above the cantilevered marble staircase leading from the lobby floor.

Right. From the exotic atmosphere of the public rooms the guest at the Nile Hilton can return to serenity in his bedroom. Natural linen, wood, and leather keep the guest rooms subdued. Tile floors help the air conditioning in making the guest forget the heat of the nearby desert. Balcony has low railing facing the river and a high wall preserving privacy of and from neighbors.

Left. A triumph in design and good taste is the 22-story Royal Hotel and S.A.S. terminal building in Copenhagen. In the two-story section are offices and shops that can be entered from both the hotel and the street. Parking is below grade.

Above. Detailing and clarity were the designer's guidelines so evident here at the front desk with its intriguing light source and the counter front of wenge used throughout the hotel for hardwood paneling. The designer's Egg chairs bring life of their own to the lobby. Covered with green hide, the swiveled chairs are grouped on rugs of greens and blues over light gray marble flooring; the acoustical tile ceiling is dark gray-green. The welded steel staircase leading to the public rooms is hung on steel rods, carpeted in emerald green, and painted white on the underside.

Facing page. The Royal's snack bar as viewed from the glass-enclosed tropical garden which is two stories high and created by double-glazed glass walls. The air conditioned garden reaches to a skylight. Tropical plants hang in the four-foot space between the glazings.

ROYAL HOTEL, COPENHAGEN, DENMARK

Architecture: Arne Jacobsen
Photography: Strüwing

97

Above. Ceiling domes in the restaurant are fitted with a lighting fixture that appears to be an upside-down collection of goblets behind which natural light is also admitted. Columns supporting the free-standing hotel tower are finished with white enamel. The imposing chairs are covered with hide.

Fluorescent tubes shielded by diffusing panels spill a welcoming pool of light at each doorway in guest room corridors. Ceiling height is only 7 feet 1½ inches. Walls are covered with fabric.

Paneling in the bedrooms is of wenge designed to a modular system that matches the wall-hung drawer units containing vanity, telephone, desk, and luggage rack. These may be hooked into the paneling whenever the guest wishes. The light fixture, invented by Arne Jacobsen, slides along its groove to where it is needed most in the room. Color schemes are combinations of soft blues and greens. The Ant chair on the left is a cousin to Jacobsen's Swan and Egg designs.

98

Above. A planter divides the working area of a guest suite from its reception area. The desk lighting fixture is of spun copper.

Below. In the Panorama lounge on the 20th floor the spun copper lighting fixture is of Oregon pine. Carpeting and upholstery are in two-tone blue. Here Jacobsen's Swan chairs are used.

CARLTON TOWER HOTEL, LONDON, ENGLAND

Architecture: Michael Rosenauer
Interiors: Henry End Associates
Photography: Alexandre Georges

Left. The Carlton Tower by night with an eight-story main wing and a 16-story tower overlooking the gardens of Cadogan Place in one of London's most fashionable neighborhoods.

Above. Focal point of the Carlton Tower lobby is the glass mural of London by Felix Topolski. Contemporary furnishings are grouped about area carpets of sandstone chenille on a floor of Italian marble. Lobby columns are faced with Bombay rosewood.

Top right. All suites at the Carlton Tower are in monochromatic schemes of gold or pewter and the latter was used for this living room in the penthouse. The 13-foot sofa is biscuit tufted in champagne silk. From the balcony, guests enjoy a sweeping view of London.

Right. The bar of the cocktail lounge is made of oak with counter inserts of black granite. This view of the lounge is from the Rib Room. Both black and white chairs are covered in leather. The off-white curtains have a bottom border of stripes in pink, black, silver, gold, and red.

The Ritz is one of the most luxurious hotels in the world with a staff of 500 for its 300 rooms. The building is faced with light gray limestone and the window walls are deeply recessed to provide large balconies. The 16-story hotel is built on Rodrigo da Fonseca Avenue, overlooking Eduardo VII Park.

Above. Art plays a major role in all the public rooms of the hotel. Hanging in the staircase off the main lounge is a tapestry of the explorer era by Lino Antonio. The green bronze statue on black marble is by Lagao Henriques. A green carpet is laid over the beige marble floor.

Below. The architecture is in the contemporary international style, but not the interiors of the bedrooms. Here we see a frankly romantic setting with four-poster beds, pink-beige walls, and a light gray and blue carpet specially woven for the room. The 20th Century traveler might have difficulty with the period dressing table. Even in a more modern vein the interiors have a dated look.

HOTEL RITZ, LISBON, PORTUGAL

Architecture and Interiors: Manuel Rodrigues,
        Fundacao Ricardo, Espirito
        Santo e Silva, Castro Freire,
        Fred Kradolfer, Lucien Donnat,
        Henry Samuel

HOTEL PHOENICIA,
BEIRUT, LEBANON

Architecture: Edward Durrel Stone
Interiors: Walter Ballard Inc.
Photography: Issa Freres

Above. Marble was used extensively in the main lobby for floor and walls. Focal point is center stone fountain and lighting fixture of iron and brass. Colors for accent are reds, pinks, orange, and violet.

Left. Four color schemes were used for the guest rooms each of which measures 16 x 12 feet. All furnishings were made in Beirut of teak with white trim and hardware of gold plated brass.

ISTANBUL HILTON,
ISTANBUL, TURKEY

Architecture: Skidmore, Owings & Merrill;
                 Associated, Sedad H. Eldem
Interiors: Jane Kidder, Hilton staff

In the exotic land of Turkey with its bulbous mosques and slender minarets, the Hilton hotel presents the stark look of the contemporary architecture that is international. The entrance canopy which is like the legendary flying carpet is the lone romantic feature of the exterior design. The 300-room hotel sits atop a hill overlooking a city park.

FORESTA HOTEL, STOCKHOLM, SWEDEN

Architecture: Hack Kampmann
Interiors: Susanne Wasson-Tucker and
Maurice Holland

Overleaf. There is not an unruly line or feature to be seen as one approaches the entrance to the Foresta Hotel. Converted from a mock castle built at the end of the 19th Century, it offers today service that meets a world-wide standard while retaining the understatement of good taste that is distinctly Scandinavian. The sign is typical of the hotel's excellent graphics. Cantilevered canopy moves inward to become the lobby ceiling. Entry is double-doored cube bisecting the glass wall facade. The white terrazzo staircase visible in the right background is cantilevered from a brick wall of glazed turquoise and beneath is a garden of gravel and potted palms. The grille of ceiling height is stainless steel.

Below. White fiber glass drapery at the far end of the lobby covers a bright yellow wall. Furniture is chalked oak and covered in a persimmon. Flooring is black terrazzo.

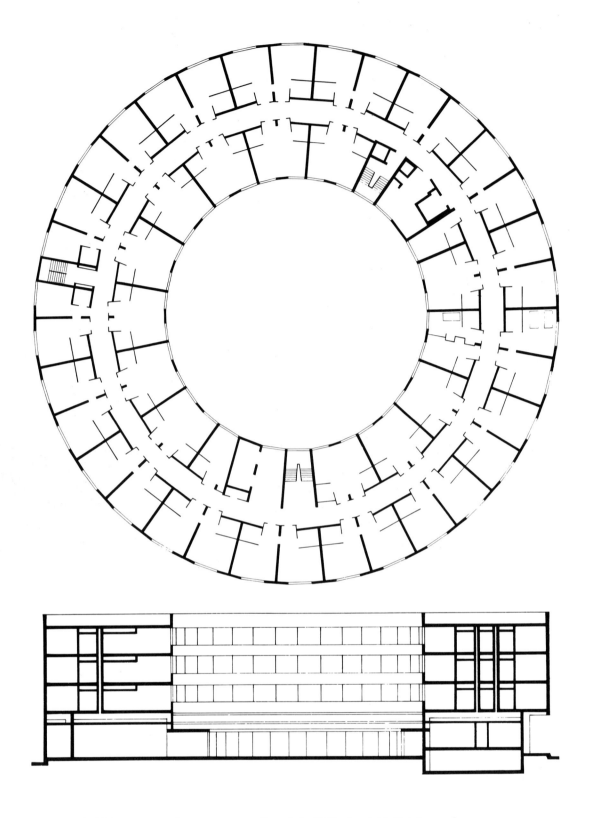

ARIEL HOTEL, LONDON, ENGLAND

Architecture: Russell Diplock Associates
         F. J. Wills and Son, Consultants

Opened in 1960, the Ariel Hotel near London's Airport was the first round hotel built in Europe and the first to offer guests individual control of air conditioning. Exterior is white mosaic with top and bottom beams finished in black crushed stone. Below is a cross-section of the hotel. Top is a typical upper floor with an outer ring of double rooms that connect and an inner ring of single rooms. The building is 176 feet in diameter, 48 feet high with 186 rooms on the upper three floors. Main restaurant designed by Sam Horwitz of Chicago seats more than 100 guests.

SHERATON TEL-AVIV, TEL-AVIV, ISRAEL

Architecture: Witkover and Baumann
Interiors: Blumenfeld and Heskin
Photography: A. Berger

This hotel was the first one built abroad by the Sheraton Corporation. It is within a short distance of the city center and is constructed of white limestone with 200 guest rooms.

Above. The main entrance has few other materials to detract from the massive impression of the limestone structure.

Left. Outstanding feature of the hotel's interior is the sculptured wall that separates this lounge from the reception hall. Israeli artist Nehemiah Azaz used plaster blocks coated with cement to create an imaginary excavation of the six civilizations that preceded the founding of ancient Palestine.

CURACAO INTERCONTINEN-
TAL HOTEL, WILLEMSTAD,
NETHERLANDS ANTILLES

Architecture and Interiors: Joseph Salerno,
                              Richard S. Smith;
                              Ben Schmit,
                              Associate Architect

Photography: Fischer

Above. This is a right-angled, three-story
structure enclosing a two-level patio which
has a garden on the lower level and a pool
terrace on the upper one. The facade of the
hotel (see page 78) is quite formal and rem-
iniscent of the Dutch homeland. The arches
here and on the terrace side of the dining
room (visible on facing page) are inspired
by the structure of the surrounding fortress
wall overlooking the sea. Tracings of this design can also be seen in the shape of the
swimming pool and the windows of the second-level guest rooms.

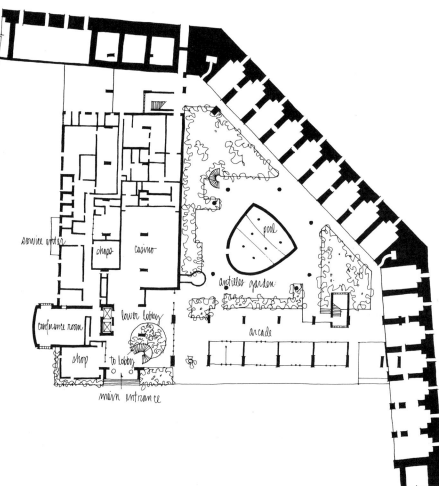

This page. Pool deck is connected by bridges with a dining terrace (at right) and a seawall promenade (left). The pool is suspended over the Antilles Garden (partly visible in the upper picture) which can be reached by the spiraling concrete staircase. Rooftops are red and the walls are pink as a result of the coral which was used as aggregate in the concrete mix.

EL SALVADOR INTERCONTI-
NENTAL HOTEL,
SAN SALVADOR, BAHAMAS

Architecture: William B. Tabler
Interiors: Robert Martin Engelbrecht

El Salvador was one of the first resort hotels designed to separate the noise-producing public rooms, restaurants, lounges, and shops from the guest room tower. Here Tabler has grouped the public areas in low buildings almost divorced from the main portion of the hotel. Fences and landscaping screen the terraces and pool deck from the street.

Because the guest rooms are relatively small with low ceilings, the designer kept the furniture to sill height and used narrow lamps so as not to obstruct the picture window view. The white ceramic balcony grille protects against prying eyes from below without blocking the view from the room.

EL PANAMA HILTON, PANAMA CITY, PANAMA

Architecture: Edward Durrel Stone;
                Associates, Mendes and Sander
Interiors: Florence Hayward
Photography: Ezra Stoller

The eggcrate facade of El Panama on a hilltop overlooking Panama City pioneered the pattern for the international style of hotel architecture that was formalized in the 1950's. Except at the center core, the hotel is only one room thick with an open-air corridor at the north side and deepset balconies shown here on the south facade.

Materials and furnishings for the terraces were chosen to create exotic and tropical atmospheres. Furniture here was designed by the architect.

113

ROYAL HOTEL,
BUDAPEST, HUNGARY

Architecture and Interiors: Sando Miko,
Istvan Verpeleti
and Kovacsy Laszlo

An astonishing success was achieved in the reconstruction of the Royal Hotel by three young Hungarian architects with no previous hotel experience.

Above. Hand-knotted carpets defining seating areas (to rear right and rear left) on the marble lobby floor were specially designed by the architects and made from undyed wool of black and gray Racka sheep. The $8 million project provided 367 rooms, all but 50 with private baths, making the Royal one of the truly modern hotels in Europe.

Right. The architects called upon the artists of Hungary for paintings and sculpture. Here in an outdoor garden café is a lifesize figure by Janos Konyorcsik. Miko designed all the furniture and prototypes were made by high school art students.

V—MOTOR HOTELS

It becomes more difficult with each year to discover the difference between the hotel and the motel.

Twenty years ago one could point to the Dew Drop Inn cottages on one hand and the Palmer House on the other. But comparisons are no longer simple when in mid-Manhattan there is a 21-story Sheraton Motor Inn with 450 rooms and an 18-story Holiday Inn with 606 rooms. The first Holiday Inn, built in Memphis in 1952, was a one-story structure with 120 rooms. The one in Manhattan a decade later was designed to handle convention sessions of 500 delegates and banquets for 400 guests.

It has underground parking for 400 cars, interior garden retreats and a rooftop swimming pool. This last item has become a must for the intown motor hotel. Five minutes after the guests check in after a day of turnpike driving they are in their bathing suits and looking for the elevator marked "To the Pool."

In one recent year 179 motor hotels were built and there probably was not a Dew Drop Inn among them. The motor hotel is big business now, no longer the Ma and Pa plan for retirement in a house by the side of the road. The American Hotel Association reports that the construction of 22,286 new motor hotel rooms in 1961 represented a capital investment of $211,458,000.

For the interior designer, the fantastic growth of the motel business has not been particularly significant because, with some rare exceptions, motor hotels have been speculative ventures by investors interested in getting the doors open with the least amount of dollars. They quickly fall into the hands of contract houses that are interested in selling furniture, not in interior design. These firms have seized most of the motor hotel business because they can provide the owners with financing for the furnishings. The designer with only his artistic skill to offer has not so far been able to compete against this lure.

Today's motels bear about as much relation to the old tourist cabin as the Baths of Caracella do to a penny arcade.

Time Magazine

And, in fact, there is some truth to the view that the average interior designer does not know how to go about buying inexpensive furniture to fit the tight budget set for most motels. It is a big problem because so many designers are simply not aware of the sources. They rarely attend the shows in High Point, Grand Rapids, or Chicago. They do not know how to shop like the contract houses do. Most interior designers would have to refuse the job when faced with the problem of finding furnishings for a motel room on a $600 budget. And indeed it is difficult to compete with the package dealers at that kind of price. Unfortunately, the net result is one more series of ugly scars on the face of America.

When the owner of a motel (as we shall call it from here on) does employ an experienced architect and a good interior designer, the result stands out in the sea of mediocre buildings that has swept across the American highway system.

MOTEL ON THE MOUNTAIN

A remarkable example of good planning, inside and out, is the Motel on the Mountain at Ramapo Pass in Suffern, N. Y. It started right at the entrepreneur, former *Time* and *Life* Magazine Bureau Chief Robert Schwartz, who had been delighted with the hillside inns of the Far East. To insure that same feeling in the motel he planned on a fifty-acre mountain top overlooking the New York Thruway, Schwartz hired Junzo Yoshimura, who had designed the Japanese house built in the courtyard of New York's Museum of Modern Art, as consultant (see illustrations, page 125).

The result was a cluster of buildings light in scale, nestled into the hillside, and sheltered by overhanging roofs. It is the Japanese approach to design: with plenty of style. The guestrooms are gracious and uncluttered; the bathrooms as luxurious as any I have ever seen.

Throughout the Motel on the Mountain, architect and designer succeeded with the use of natural materials and simple colors; headboards of oiled walnut, desks and nightstands topped with white mica, benches of cherry and steel, and wall coverings of grays, blacks, whites, and golds.

It is unfortunate that Motel on the Mountain should be such a rare commodity in a time when so many motels are being built. Most of these are involved with chain operations and with franchises, so there is little use in looking for exceptional concept and design.

HOWARD JOHNSON

Rufus Nims, the Miami architect who did some of the original research on motels for the Howard Johnson management in the early 1950s, was one of the first to spot the trend toward moribund design in the industry. Interviewed during the development of this chapter, Nims made the point that banks have no facilities for evaluating individual effort and the ability to create a motel that will perform properly. He made the point that:

> They lean to the chain name and trademarks because this gives
> them a feeling of security, a comforting thought that the operators
> will be able to make the payments on the mortgage.

A banker does not lend money on a motel because of its design. He has neither the time nor, probably, the talent to bother with this aspect of the building. All he wants to see is the financial statement and the credit rating of the man who is going to sign the mortgage. Nims says he learned a long time ago that it does no good to have a client with a great awareness of design, public taste, and proper management if the man does not have a heavy financial statement. Without the last the client may actually be penalized in his effort to find financing. Thus, the chain motel has great appeal to the investor. But with a chain motel, as with any kind of political or financial empire, there must be strong direction from the top. There must be regimentation and a consequent reduction to a predictable quality. Nims points out that

> the Howard Johnson restaurant, for instance, has no obligation
> to be the best restaurant in a neighborhood, only to be predictable.

But there are some definite advantages built into any system of mass merchandising. When a strict code of operation is set up, the need for exceptional employees is reduced. Let us say the franchise operator of a motel hires a lodge brother to design the building and gets his sister-in-law to buy the furnishings. Unless he is a complete idiot, he will stay out of serious trouble because of the rules and regulations set up by the mother organization. Specifications are set out so that the rankest architect cannot go too far wrong. Experience has provided a pretty good idea of what costs should run. In Nims' view, the worst thing about the system is that neither the architect nor designer can ever go beyond what they know today, which is already a couple years out of date. The chain operation only refines the details and faults of the past, holding to the predictability instead of reconnoitering for what the public might like better.

WARM MINERAL SPRINGS

One of the remarkably different motels built during the 1950s was Warm Mineral Springs Inn at Venice on the west coast of Florida. It was designed by Victor Lundy of Sarasota and was one of the projects that created a national reputation for the young architect.

It took 75 concrete shells set on precast stems to create twenty units, plus an office. Cost ran under $160,000. The striking form of the mushroom-shaped units was repeated in the roadside sign so that architecture, not a great flashing of neon, created the welcome (see illustrations, page 128).

The furnishings show no attempt to match the high quality of the exterior design. Yet the interplay of light and shadow from the roof patterns, plus the mahogany veneered plywood, make for an interesting atmosphere. The roof shells provide a generous overhang to shield the sliding glass doors of the rooms from sun and from the frequent tropical showers. The motel has great appeal from the road, but Nims is probably correct in assuming that the developer did not get fifty cents extra for design from the bank.

Today, every smart hotel operator has recognized the importance of developing motor inns at strategic locations downtown, at turnpike terminals, and at airports. The chains employ specialists who do nothing but scout the future programs of federal and state road departments in search of clues to good locations. Hundreds of options on land are taken on the basis of turnpike projections.

THE NIMS-KOCH-WOODWARD RESEARCH

But it was the Howard Johnson organization that was first to foresee the coming public demand for quality accommodations along our highways. Nims in Miami and Carl Koch at Massachusetts Institute of Technology near the Howard Johnson headquarters in Boston were both hired to do basic research into room types and combinations and on furnishings and finishes. Funds were not unlimited, but between them the two architects came up with a prototype room that raised motel standards for the country. Though there are many grand motels around the country today, the Howard Johnson Lodge is still used as a measuring rod. People tend to say that a motel is either better or worse than a Howard Johnson one.

Nims, Koch, and the management of Howard Johnsons all recognized a danger in making the motel room so luxurious that the price would get beyond that which people expected to spend for a night's lodging. The secret of Howard Johnson's success with the restaurant is that their appearance gives a pretty good idea of what it will cost to eat there.

With its early motels, Johnson learned that the couple paying twelve dollars for a double room at the Johnson Lodge would look for a better place to eat than the Howard Johnson restaurant. This discovery bore out Nims' original theory that Howard Johnson would be forced someday to use another name for restaurants adjoining its fancier motor lodges.

One of the early prototype rooms by Nims and Koch featured sloping headboard for comfortable reading in bed, and a continuous plastic-topped counter incorporating desk, television stand, and luggage rack. Much of the research for interiors of these early rooms was done in collaboration with John Woodward, president of Contract Interiors of Boston.

The three men did not win all the arguments, but they did achieve the covered walkways that tie buildings together and make it possible for the motorist to unload his car in the rain without getting too wet. They pushed the idea that people were living more out of suitcases, and that luggage racks were a better idea than casegoods. This is still true, not only of motels but also for the downtown hotel. But care must be taken to evaluate the individual characteristics of a location.

A stock plan for every motel between Maine and Arizona is impossible; careful analysis will always turn up essential differences. But this factor is usually overlooked in the chain operation. For instance, one Howard Johnson Lodge in Palm Beach includes the required luggage rack, but nobody had stopped to consider that people coming to a resort area bring along extra clothes and need extra room to hang and shelve them. It's a perfect example of the dangers inherent in the stock plan.

The Nims-Koch-Woodward research turned up some clues to the probably behavior of motel guests. The guest moves from the car to the luggage rack, then to the dressing area, past the bed and through the sitting area to the view from window or sliding glass doors. Between the dressing area and bedroom, the architects devised a partial screen, sometimes slats of cedar, to provide organization to the unit and some amount of privacy for the guest without cutting off light and air.

Considering the short history of the motel, it is remarkable that the business took only three decades to go from the primitive wood cabin to the glossy resort with swimming pools, cocktail lounges, and fancy restaurants. The big problem with the early motels was that the owners had little or no experience in playing Mine Host. Some of them may have been successful businessmen, but mostly along lines unrelated to putting people up for the night. When Howard Johnson started its research program, the majority of people getting into the motel business knew none of the fundamentals. They had no idea what it cost to wash a sheet or clean a wall, maintain a bathroom or a parking area. There was never any carpeting in motels because it was assumed that hard floors were cheaper to maintain; one of the first things Nims and Koch learned from hotel men was that it was cheaper to clean a carpet. But despite the research, the architects found the industry unwilling to accept their findings. As businessmen, motel

The average guest hopes he will not be involved in a lot of tipping in a motel, yet part of his luggage, and sometimes enough for the whole family, must get from the car to the room. So parking should be as convenient to his quarters as possible.

John Carden Campbell, AIA
Architectural Record

U. S. motels, once thought of as only a place to lay down one's head overnight, are competing with one another to give Americans the most outlandishly luxurious and wildly gimmicked night's rest in the history of the middle class.

Time Magazine

owners were used to making their own decisions and, like most amateurs, they were more often wrong than right. It was not until the chains brought in experienced hotel men that the motels began to make economic sense.

END OF THE MA AND PA ERA

The smart operators quickly realized that the properly planned and operated motel was literally a gold mine, capable of returning as high as 25% on an investment. Growth came quickly then. In 1957, the average new motel had twenty rooms. Five years later, the number had climbed to nearly fifty. The Ma and Pa cottages that remain today exist only because the owners can't sell out and are not sophisticated enough to know how to go into bankruptcy. What used to be a means of stretching income in the Golden Years has become as dynamic a part of our economy as the supermarket.

In the Neanderthal stage of the motel business only a decade ago, the owner went to the cheapest furniture store in town and bargained for a wholesale price on beds, chests, nightstands . . . as few items as he figured he could get away with.

Do you know why you never saw a bathtub in those early-day motels? Because the motels had such a bad reputation that nobody would have dared sit in a tub. In most of the gangster movies the hideout was usually a grimy motel. Nor should one overlook the stigma of the "hot pillow" trade. Considering that background, the motel has changed as radically as Eliza Doolittle, heroine of George Bernard Shaw's *Pygmalion* and Lerner and Loewe's *My Fair Lady*.

The resort motels of South Florida, California, and Las Vegas had a great influence in forcing an upgrading of interior design. The traveling salesman often finds turnpike driving is better for short distances than the airplane. He expects a cheerful room when he checks into a motel. So does everybody else on the highway. Motorists stop earlier in the afternoon because they have come to anticipate a few pleasant hours before turning in for the night. Therefore, the bedrooms of a motel must be made more cheerful than those at home, none too difficult a task in view of the dreariness of the average American bedroom. It is usually the last room in the house to be furnished in any kind of style. It is certainly the room that suffers the most from clutter. It is probably true that many a man goes back to work sooner than he should after an illness because he is so tired of looking at the four walls of his bedroom.

Another important factor in the demand for high quality of design is the current high living standard. The traveling businessman and the family on vacation do not expect to lower their standard of living. They actually expect a higher one than they have at home.

The grand motel represents an attempt to combine the do-it-yourself, open shirted ease of the older motel with the facilities of the luxury hotel. The four senior citizens playing gin rummy in their undershirts beside a motel swimming pool would probably feel uncomfortable in a more elegant establishment.

Fortune Magazine

MOTEL DE VILLE

One of the first results of this new approach within the industry was the Motel de Ville with 150 rooms in downtown New Orleans (see illustrations, page 132). Nobody connected with the project had had motel experience but the idea was sound: to build a motel with all of the facilities of a good hotel. The developer was Shelby Construction Company which has background in real estate and apartment buildings. The architect was Charles R. Colbert, who later became Dean of the Architectural School of Columbia University. Our office, largely because of its work at the time at the Muehlebach Hotel in Kansas City, was hired for the interior design.

The job was an exciting one from the start and everyone connected with the project was satisfied. Due to the fact that it was planned from a hotel point of view, the Motel de Ville achieved a more lasting quality. When most motel rooms were being furnished for $600, Shelby set a budget of $1,500.

The money was used to buy better, not more, furniture and the policy proved a good one. Occupancy has run at an average well over 90% and the furnishings look as fresh and contemporary today as they did when the de Ville opened. The case goods and chairs were made of natural walnut with matching plastic-laminate tops. Hardware fixtures were of brass and finished bronze. Room interiors were white except for an accent wall of wood paneling and one short window wall covered with handprinted drapery coordinated with the particular scheme of the room. There were three distinct schemes: Siamese pink-turquoise-black-white; copper-black-white; and purple-aqua-black-white.

The two floors of the H-shaped motel are on stilts to provide sheltered parking and to bring cars as close to the rooms as possible. Rooms are backed up to one another. Along the outside corridor are screens of redwood. Inside rooms have a view of two landscaped courtyards with swimming pool, play area, and wading pool for children. From the parking stalls it is a simple matter for the guest to reach his room by stairs or elevator. While this satisfies the basic requirement of a motel, the de Ville provides all the comforts of a downtown hotel. These include 24-hour room service, air-conditioning, cocktail lounge and roof terrace, restaurant, radio, and television. There are eight special suites with kitchen facilities.

The architects designed an excellent bathroom, one of the finest I have seen and one the owners plan to use in their projected motel in St. Louis. It is small, but the functionally designed one-piece wash basin and counter, plus the specially designed medicine cabinet, provide ample storage and surface area. There are no shower doors on the tub because it was found these create a feeling of insecurity in a small space. There is a psychological resistance to them on the part of the guest, probably because of a fear of slipping and falling through the glass . . . even plastic doors do nothing to reduce the uneasiness. To this problem the shower curtain rod still appears the best solution. It seemed a brilliant idea to recess the curtain rod into the bathroom ceiling, but management soon discovered this deprived women of a place to hang wet hose and underwear.

THE $100,000 TOWEL HOOK

It is so often a small thing that creates a big impression on the guest. And it can make a big impression on management. In planning its hotel in Hartford, Statler was determined to make as few mistakes as possible. A complete research program was set up by architect William Tabler and one result was a simple towel hook in the bathroom which financed $100,000-worth of construction. Research indicated that a handy wall hook would induce a guest to use a face towel four times instead of once. With 455 rooms this means a laundry saving of $20 a day, which adds up to $7,300 a year ... enough to meet interest and payments on $100,000 in capital investment.

This is the kind of saving that management is quick to appreciate. It is more difficult for the designer and architect to talk management into spending a little more now to get back a lot more later. The average motel developer is always full of fears about the location and his present and future competition. Traffic may be heavy today, but what will happen if a new highway project diverts the motorists? So there is that natural tendency to hold down costs. The architect and designer both have the obligation to create a motel that will enjoy high occupancy. If the place costs $8,000 a room instead of $7,000 and the occupancy is increased by ten or fifteen per cent, the owner will be far ahead. But these are abstract figures and nobody can prove them when all that exists is a vacant piece of property and a set of plans.

PHILADELPHIA MARRIOTT

There is nothing abstract about the success of the Philadelphia Marriott on the Main Line near Bala-Cynwyd and Merion (see illustrations, page 134). The fourth motor hotel built by the Hot Shoppes, it was designed to function both as a resort for the tourist and as a convention site for medium-sized groups. Architect Tabler so designed the eight banquet and meeting rooms that they can be thrown together to provide a ballroom for 700 persons.

The Marriott, with four buildings looking inward to a terrace and swimming pool, has proved a weekend attraction for Philadelphians anxious to get away from the house but unwilling to tackle busy highways. There are two specialty restaurants; the exotic Polynesian Kona Kai and the Sirloin and Saddle Steak Room with its great copper hooded grill and walls of weathered oak paneling. In addition, there is a coffee shop. Though designed for more simple family dining, this last nevertheless offers a warm atmosphere with carpeting, walnut paneling, and colorful Pennsylvania Dutch style paintings.

Tabler is an architect who sincerely believes a job goes better when the interior designer is brought in at the conception. In the case of the Marriott this provided the opportunity to work out the budget with emphasis on the public spaces. Money must be spent where it counts the most.

The guestrooms of the Philadelphia Marriott were adequately furnished in good taste, something between $800 and $900 a room. But in the public areas, especially the lobby, there are lavish touches. The lobby floor is Vermont slate accented by handsome handmade carpets. The walls are of Brazilian rosewood. The quilted upholstery was expensive, but there is relatively little of it so the luxury is justified. In buying several hundred chairs for the guestrooms, every effort must be made to provide an economical design and maintenance-free materials. But for those few sofas and chairs in the lobby areas, the best is not too good, for it is here that the guest gets his first impression.

Today's hotel must be a motel and had better be a resort. The line between hotel and motels, on the one hand, and resort on the other is dimming. Hotels everywhere are introducing resort appeals: swimming pools, organized recreation and most important of all — beautiful food.

James Pearson, Editor
Southern Hotel Journal

The American has sacrificed his life as a whole to the motor car, like someone who, demented with passion, wrecks his home in order to lavish his income on a capricious mistress whose promises and delights he can only occasionally enjoy.

Lewis Mumford
Architectural Record

V—MOTOR HOTELS

Illustrations

The text for this Chapter will be found on pages 117 to 123

MOTEL ON THE MOUNTAIN, SUFFERN, N. Y.

Architecture: Harwell Hamilton Harris,
          Perkins & Wills, architects of the
          guest buildings; Junzo
          Yoshimura, general architectural
          consultant, architect of
          restaurant; Steinhardt &
          Thompson, architects associated
          with Junzo Yoshimura on
          restaurant
Interiors: Leonore Schwartz
Photography: exterior, Richard Pousette-Dart
             interior, Alexandre Georges

Perched high above the New York Thruway, the Motel on the Mountain has the exquisite perfection of a Japanese flower arrangement. Against the bulk of a 50-acre mountain top the buildings have the lightness and delicacy of the Ming tree. The developer's delight with the hillside inns of Japan led him to create this motel at the Ramapo Pass 27 miles north of New York City. Lamp posts line the road which is precisely composed so that the motorists see a trail of lights circling up the mountainside. Each building is connected to another by a covered walkway on four-inch steel posts. Half of the motel units have balconies cantilevered above the granite slope.

Previous page. A view of the restaurant which is at the highest point of the hill. The structure of laminated beams has a capacity of 400 customers and covered walks extend around a garden and pool at the entry.

Top, facing page. Balcony of a typical bedroom affords a view of the mountainside and the winding Thruway in the valley.

Lower left, facing page. Sink tops in the dressing area are stoneware by David Weinrib and Karen Karnes of Stony Point.

Lower right, facing page. One continuous piece of oiled walnut is used for the headboard in this graciously proportioned suite bedroom. Desk and night stands are suspended from the wall and topped with white mica.

Below and facing page. One of the early successes of Sarasota architect Victor Lundy was the Warm Mineral Springs Inn at Venice on the Florida west coast. Here are seen the concrete parasols that Lundy used to form the office and 20 motel units. The striking design serves also for a traffic-stopping sign.

Above. In the interiors the slightly overlapping two-level hyperbolic parabaloids form clerestories.

WARM MINERAL SPRINGS INN, VENICE, FLA.

Architecture and Interiors: Victor Lundy
Photography: Alexandre Georges

It was architect Nims' theory that the name Howard Johnson should produce an instant image for the motorist seeking a place to turn in for the night. It had to add up to shelter of a known quality and a moderate price. This two-story lodge at Little Rock proved to satisfy the formula.

Right. All rooms have open beams and sand colored brick walls. On the ground floor the ceilings are level, on the second floor they are peaked. The wall-hung unit combines desk, vanity, and luggage rack and has a top of birch plastic laminate. The partial screen forming the dressing area gave the designer an opportunity to use fine Chinese wall covering as an accent. In these experimental units Nims and Woodward kept the beds unusually low to encourage guests to use them for seating. It broke an old hotel rule, but it worked.

Below right. This room follows the rule that guests will move from their car to the luggage rack (right foreground), past the dressing area (left), past the bed, and on to a sitting area to get a view from the window or patio doors. The open wire chair helps create space. The Johnson executives were suspicious of the open lavatory counter behind the screen but the customers found it handy and it has since been adopted by other designers.

HOWARD JOHNSON MOTEL, LITTLE ROCK, ARK.

Architecture: Rufus Nims
Interiors: John Woodward

HOWARD JOHNSON MOTEL, HUNTINGTON, N. Y.

Architecture: Carl Koch
Interiors: John Woodward
Photography: Louis Reens

In designing their motor lodge at Huntington the Howard Johnson chain used the weather-vaned orange and blue tower which is the trade-mark for their roadside restaurants. Each motel in the chain is located within easy reach of one of the chain restaurants.

Above. Against a wall of cinder block are the mica-topped television bench and desk. Steel strips embedded in the desk top provide a luggage rack without taking up any valuable floor space. Howard Johnson helped pioneer the shift from "casegoods." The slatted partition to separate the dressing area was another result of the chain's early research into the likes and dislikes of the motoring American. It made the room more orderly without chopping up the space into mean areas. All Howard Johnson motel rooms were carpeted when it was discovered that it was easier to maintain this type of flooring than to clean a hard surface. Frequent replacing of less costly carpeting has proved economical. In the Huntington motel, three color schemes are based on carpet colors of moss green, brown, and sand. In each room are a wall of natural mahogany, one of cinderblock, and a white ceiling with dark beams.

MOTEL DE VILLE,
NEW ORLEANS, LA.

Architecture: Charles R. Colbert
Interiors: Henry End Associates
Photography: Frank Lotz Miller

Frontispiece, page 116. Guests cannot drive to their rooms at the Motel de Ville but they can get within a flight or two of stairs. There is also an elevator to carry them to the two floors of guest rooms that are double banked. Outer corridors are shielded by verticals of redwood. Rooms facing away from the street have a view of two courtyards with swimming pool and recreation area for children.

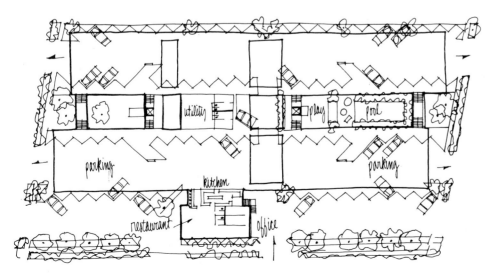

Left. This plan of the Motel de Ville shows the parking which is beneath the building so that the guests won't view a sea of cars.

Facing page. The design of the scalloped parking bays beneath the motel is picked up in the front of the ground level coffee shop. The simple wrought iron chairs have wicker backs. Screening the kitchen is translucent plastic.

Above. This is one of the eight special suites. Folding door at left closes off kitchen area.

PHILADELPHIA MARRIOTT, PHILADELPHIA, PA.

Architecture: William B. Tabler
Interiors: Henry End Associates
Photography: Robert C. Lautman

Above. The resort atmosphere of the Philadelphia Marriott attracts not only the motoring tourist, but also families from suburban Philadelphia looking for a convenient weekend vacation spot. Four buildings look inward to the pool terrace. Doors are painted in descending colors from crimson on the top floor to yellow on ground level. These colors are keyed to the linings of the draperies at the floor to ceiling windows.

Right. Here we see the impact of lavish touches in public spaces. In the lobby a red carpet marks out the seating arrangement to the left on a floor of polished Vermont slate. The walls and front desk paneling are of Brazilian rosewood. Early history of Philadelphia is portrayed in a series of paintings by Shirley Tattersfield that cover the far wall.

Pennsylvania Dutch style paintings lend a more informal look to the Fairfield Inn which serves as a coffee shop and a room for family dining. The carpet picks up the room's accent colors of citron and persimmon.

Twin bedroom has desk and luggage rack combination topped with plastic laminate. Colors throughout the guest rooms are citron, persimmon, and mocha. The motel also provides studios, suites, and combination studio/double rooms.

MARRIOTT KEY BRIDGE MOTEL, ROSSLYN, VA.

Architecture: Carlos B. Schoeppl and
Robert K. Frese
Interiors: Henry End Associates
Photography: Louis Reens

Facing page. In the lobby of the Marriott Key Bridge is a luxurious carpet in gold, beige, and tangerine with a striking wall of fieldstone. Flooring at the lobby entrance is slate.

Above. Typical studio room provides two king-size convertible sofas in pleasant living room atmosphere. Many of these rooms have paneling of walnut veneer.

Left. Plastic fret screen separates the bedroom and dressing area from living room of a suite which features wall-to-wall carpeting and a color scheme of citron, yellow, and mocha.

CHARTER HOUSE MOTOR LODGE, ANNAPOLIS, MD.

Architecture and Interiors: Victor Gruen
Associates

Above. Sheltered driveway provides a drive-up registration desk so the motorist does not have to get out of the car. In this building is a restaurant to serve the 56-unit motel that consists of three two-story buildings. These look in on a large landscaped court with a swimming pool.

Right. Rooms are simply decorated, but pick up glamor from the brilliant color schemes by Eszter Haraszty. All windows overlook the courtyard. Sleeping areas are buffered against corridor and parking lot noises by the closet and dressing room partitions. Cabinet and desk combination to the right are natural wood topped with white mica.

HILTON INN, SAN FRANCISCO, CALIF.

Architecture: William B. Tabler
Interiors: Elliott Frey

Left. Two wings, each with 151 rooms, face into a landscaped courtyard with swimming pool, wading pool, and recreational facilities for children. The Hilton Inn is built on 10 acres near the San Francisco airport. The circular building with the folded plate roof is an administration building that also contains a private club with its own swimming pool, several restaurants, and the necessary barbershop, beauty parlor, and other services for the motel guest. Parking is restricted to the outside of the building complex.

Above. Typical guest room of the Hilton Inn provides an appliance that makes two cups of complimentary coffee (shown at right beneath the wall lamps). Newer designs of the coffee maker are more pleasing. The long luggage rack against the opposite wall (left in the photograph) makes it easy to live out of a suitcase, something most tourists prefer to do.

HILTON INN, SEATTLE, WASH.

Architecture: Skidmore, Owings & Merrill
Interiors: public spaces, Roland Terry; guest
rooms, David T. Williams, A.I.D.

Facing page. The spirit of the rugged northwest is embodied in the strong elements employed by designer Roland Terry. Here at the north end of the lobby that leads to the guest rooms are flagstone flooring and heavy beams of Douglas fir. Hilton never neglects to utilize the talent of local artists and craftsmen to lend authentic color. Throughout the Seattle inn are murals, paintings, abstract sculpture in metal, wood, and plaster, and panels. The painting in the background here in the lobby is by John Herard.

Above. Indoors and out are joined where the lobby meets the glass-enclosed atrium on three sides. Custom rugs atop a floor of flagstone define seating areas in the lobby. The ceiling is slatted fir and the far wall is a vertigris panel by Roland Terry. The trio of abstract forms is by James Wegner who also created the brushed terrazzo flooring for the pool.

Right. The bar and dining room look onto a garden walled with Montana slate. Custom tables have mica tops and the chairs are upholstered in gold plastic.

GOLFOTEL, MID-PINES
COUNTRY CLUB,
MOORE COUNTY, N. C.

Architecture and Interiors: Thomas T. Hayes, Jr.
Photography: Molitor

A motel for golfers was designed by Thomas
T. Hayes, Jr. at the Mid-Pines Country Club
in Moore County, North Carolina. The eight
double bedrooms are laid out in a sawtooth
manner to provide each unit with a small
entrance court and a semi-private area of the
deck overlooking a lake; the latter is made
full use of by means of a glass wall with
bottom opening for ventilation. For large
family groups or business sessions, the inter-
connecting rooms can be used in combination.
With the "golfotel" perched on the edge of
the course, golfers can walk in from the fair-
way to wash up in their own room. There is
thus no bother with locker room changing.

MARK THOMAS INN,
MONTEREY, CALIF.

Architecture: John Carl Warnecke
Interiors: James Aldrich
Landscape architecture: Laurence Halprin
Photography: Morley Baer

Facing page, Lobby of the Mark Thomas Inn is small, yet the architect and designer have achieved space through a strong expression of the materials and a careful disposition of seating areas. This conversation area is composed of a cocoa rug against a deep reddish brown of the waxed concrete floor. Bertoia chairs in vivid blues and greens attend a rattan table with Kappa shell top. Beams and paneling are redwood.

Restful atmosphere of the rooms is evident in these photographs of a twin bedroom and a spacious double. In each room is an accent wall of grass cloth in the medium tone of one of three color schemes throughout the inn: olive and orange; purple, cerise, and pink; lemon, blue-green, and spruce blue. All other walls are off-white. The designer drew upon the years he lived in Mexico. Grillework at the foyer and the antique brass of the lamp stands provide touches of a foreign flavor. So do the gouaches by Pepe Gomez and the hand-blocked muslin draperies that repeat the pattern of the grilles.

The 320-room International Hotel perches above bright blue columns, making it appear to float above its ten-acre site. Built in 1958, it was one of the first hotels designed to catch the air traveler before he started the long ride to downtown. But it also has the facilities and glamor to attract a clientele should technical advances make it possible to airlift travelers easily to mid-city. The hotel was extensively landscaped and the service area at lower left was carefully screened by a pierced block wall. Mindful of the jet roar from bigger and bigger engines, architect Tabler used half-inch thick glass for the picture windows that extend the width of the guest room. Plan of a typical floor of guest rooms in the International Hotel shows how picture windows for pairs of rooms are spaced between columns. The plan does not show layout of larger suites.

In the guest rooms walnut furniture is in a Scandinavian scale of design. The hi-fi and stereo components were designed by Thomas W. Ulrichs of the Cudlipp office.

INTERNATIONAL HOTEL, IDLEWILD AIRPORT, NEW YORK, N. Y.

Architecture: William B. Tabler
Interiors: public rooms, Dorothy Draper, Inc.
　　　　　guest rooms, Chandler Cudlipp
　　　　　& Associates

146

VI – REJUVENATING THE OBSOLETE

Illustrations

The text for this Chapter will be found on pages 173 to 186

THE PLAZA, NEW YORK, N. Y.

Interiors: Henry End Associates
Associate: Ninette Mulvany
Photography: Ezra Stoller

Built more than half a century ago, the Plaza today remains the truly grand hotel of the United States. Inside, a never-ending effort at keeping the hotel up-to-date. The picture on page 148 shows an austere building of another age gazing across Central Park.

Above. Original painted door panels were retained in the corridor of the Terrace ballroom on the 58th Street side of the hotel. The old crimson gave way to a new color scheme of white, gold, persimmon, and a blending of black and white in the new carpet. Also new are the planters, benches and the Louis XVI panels above the doors.

Top, facing page. One of the refurbished bedrooms with new furniture, new carpeting and flocked wallpaper in a Renaissance pattern. The window treatment serves to emphasize the expanse of the window. Three color schemes were used: pewter, melon, and gold, varying slightly from room to room.

Right. The gracious life provided at the Plaza is exemplified in this dining area of a corner suite.

Over. The famous Terrace Room of the Plaza lost its crimson velour draperies and upholsteries and gained a brighter look with persimmon ones. The three chandeliers in the main room were left alone, but those on the balconies were enlarged. Only architectural additions were the carved ebony pineapples on bronze bases over the white balustrades. The coffered paneling and painted panels on the ceilings and walls were simply cleaned to restore their 1911 luster.

151

PRINCE CONTI HOTEL, NEW ORLEANS, LA.

Architecture: Eugene Gilbert
Interiors: Charles Gresham, A.I.D.
Photography: Leon Trice

Once a warehouse, the Prince Conti has been changed into a gracious hotel. It has so much Old World charm that one would guess it had been receiving guests for a century. The original brick facade has been dressed up with the typical French Quarter arched windows, black iron grille, and copper lanterns. The iron gate at right is the motor entrance.

All bedrooms are furnished with antiques and so no two are alike. White on white flocked wall paper is used in the Prince Conti Room. The carved headboard is from Austria and the marble night tables are Italian imports. Carpet is green and the draperies are gold.

AMBASSADOR HOTEL'S COCOANUT GROVE, LOS ANGELES, CALIF.

Interiors: Henry End Associates;
Photography: Robert C. Cleveland

Above. The Cocoanut Grove supper club reaped its just reward of an exotic face-lifting. Here at the entrance, antique blackamoors light the guest's way. White Moroccan screens are lighted from behind. The beige and black vinyl floor is outlined in brass.

Left. Hundreds of lighting fixtures were recessed in the acoustical ceiling of deep blue to create the theatrical lighting. This is a view of the entrance to the exotic room.

HOTEL NEW ORLEANS, NEW ORLEANS, LA.

Architecture: Curtis & Davis
Photography: Frank Lotz Miller

Right. A startling face lifting of this old hotel was achieved with a brick veneer wall 32 feet high, a re-designed sign, and a mosaic tile facing for the existing canopy. Even the newspaper stand on the sidewalk was glamorized with a mica covering. The brick was pierced in front of windows.

Above. A new terrazzo floor and contemporary furnishings have transformed the lobby and made it appear larger though, in fact, the space was reduced to provide for a larger kitchen and mezzanine. The sheer drapery at left was designed by the architects and backlighted to create a feeling of space behind it. The columns are faced with white mica. Registration counter, at rear, is faced with a redwood plywood and topped with mica.

Facing page. Against the background of a charcoal gray ceiling, a 60-foot-long chandelier of brass rods gleams and twinkles like a strange constellation in the lobby.

SHERATON CHICAGO, CHICAGO, ILL.

Architecture: Quinn & Christiansen, in
collaboration with Sheraton
Corporations architectural and
engineering departments
Interiors: Mary Morrison Kennedy, A.I.D.

Above. To attract Chicago's carriage trade, the design staff was given a lavish budget for the top floor suites of the new building. Japanese ladies stroll across the long wall. At both ends of the room are walls covered in a glistening bronze wallpaper. Flanking the sofa bed at the far end are lamps inspired by antique brass altar candlesticks. Carpet is olive green chenille.

Left. Here again a subtle touch of the Oriental in furnishings and wall decoration. Wallpaper in the room is a mosaic in gray and gold and the carpet is gray.

Facing page. The 42-story Sheraton on Michigan Avenue in Chicago had excellent facilities but only 500 rooms, too few to support the hotel in high style. The answer was the handsome 25-story addition (left foreground) which added 600 rooms. The older building was steam cleaned and a new entrance was placed between the two.

SHERMAN HOTEL,
CHICAGO, ILL.

Interiors: Everett Brown Associates
Photography: Hedrich-Blessing

Above. House on the Roof, the re-designed
penthouse erected on the roof of the Hotel
Sherman is one of the truly luxurious pent-
houses in the world of hotel life. Extending
the length of the penthouse on the lower level
is a glass-enclosed solarium. Edwardian wicker
chairs alternate with more delicate ones in
wrought iron. At top, right, is a glimpse of
the large yellow Japanese lanterns strung the
length of the room. The room has a feeling of
eternal summer 24 floors above Chicago's loop.

Right. The entrance hall features this three-
story spiraling staircase that is free-hanging
Walls are covered in lavender wool suede and
the carpeting is scarlet. On the second floor
are a living room, kitchen big enough to
handle a small banquet, foyer, bar, and solarium. Four bedrooms are on the upper floor.

SHERATON EAST,
NEW YORK, N. Y.

Interiors: Michael Greer, N.S.I.D.

Top. Living room of one of the refurbished Sheraton East suites features white silk wall covering with olive green flocking. One of the wing chairs is an antique and the other is a reproduction. Most of the furnishings are reproductions, but there are genuine touches such as the figurines on the mantle, the brass firescreen, and the marble clock which were purchased from the Governor Fuller estate in Massachusetts.

Left. This combination bed-sitting room is one of a series of one-room suites in the hotel and, like the rest of the guest rooms, has a French tone to its furnishings.

BROADMOOR HOTEL,
COLORADO SPRINGS, COLO.

Interiors: Leslie Dorsey, W. & J. Sloane
Photography: Benschneider

Above right. The Broadmoor was built on the banks of a man-made lake in 1918. The architects were Whitney & Warren who also designed Grand Central Station in New York.

Lower right. In the refurbishing of this famous resort it was decided to emphasize the continental atmosphere. In the ballroom corridor, to which this is the entrance, lighting dramatizes the original painted arched ceiling. The carpet is a deep blue and gold and natural greenery hangs from the chandelier.

Top, facing page. The ceiling of the Oval Room of the Broadmoor's golf clubhouse resembles an exploding star with stripes of blue, gold, turquoise, and white. The room was used as a casino in its early days when Colorado Springs was popular with European society.

Bottom, facing page. The sun lounge is arranged around an old Italian fountain and lit from white plaster urns and pedestals. The paneling and wall lights from before the redecorating were kept, as was the ceiling although the latter was painted yellow and white.

162

**KENILWORTH HOTEL,
BAL HARBOUR, FLA.**

Interiors: Henry End Associates
Photography: Ezra Stoller

Above. While other hotels on the Florida Gold Coast were trimming their sails to meet competition, the Kenilworth redesigned its guest rooms to upgrade them. This typical bedroom illustrates the efforts at sumptuosness.

Facing page. New furnishings with clean lines and low scale succeed in overcoming the stiff march of marble columns in the lobby of this oceanside hotel.

Below. No fountains, no Dresden figurines, no nymphs in the lounge of the Kenilworth. Only decorations are the murals by Shirley Tattesfield, the window treatment, and the palms.

165

SAVOY-HILTON,
NEW YORK, N. Y.

Interiors: Tom Lee, Ltd.

Photography: top, Alexandre Georges
bottom, Ernie Silva

The focal point of the Savoy bar is the plastic mural by Peter Ostine, back-lit like a stained glass window. General lighting for the bar is by recessed spot. Seating and bar edge are leather covered.

KENMORE HOTEL, BOSTON, MASS.

Interiors: Roland Jutras, N.S.I.D.
Photography: Louis Reens

Hearty remodelling of the hotel's Viking Room to the Beef 'n Bird restaurant produced encouraging results on the auditor's report. With wood paneling and old brick, Roland Jutras of the Hotel Corporation of America design staff created the atmosphere of an old English country restaurant. The $60,000 investment pushed quarterly food and drink business from $54,000 to $95,000. Carving counter for beef ribs is set in the brick wall at right in the lower picture under an antiqued pewter hood. Carpet is in reds and blacks.

Wood from a 150-year-old New England barn was used for the paneling. Other atmospheric changes came from a collection of English seals and prints. Lanterns are bronze with amber cathedral glass. Leather chairs alternate with cane-backed ones.

HOTEL NAVARRO,
NEW YORK, N. Y.

Interiors: Henry End Associates
Photography: Louis Reens, Alexandre Georges

Above. Elevator lobby was cramped, but more space was an impossibility. A solution was found with the mirrored wall and the backlighted translucent screen that creates an illusion of space beyond. Stained glass disks in five colors are set at random in the rings of brass. White leather covers the brass benches.

Right. Formerly when a guest stood in the small vestibule he was confronted by a ceiling that was a jumble of beams and pilasters. In the remodeling of the lobby, the ceiling was dropped and the chandelier installed. Furniture was kept small and low. At far end is the small elevator lobby.

Facing page. The Navarro has extraordinarily large suites but the former furnishings did not warrant the rates required by economics. The living areas now present a picture of residential comfort and relaxation. In the suite shown in the upper picture, the color scheme is gold; in the one shown below it the scheme is blue and green. Pink and beige are the two other variants.

FAIRMONT HOTEL, SAN FRANCISCO, CALIF.

Architecture: Mario Gaidano, A.I.A.
Interiors: Barbara Dorn, A.I.D.
Photography: Eugene Anthony

Above. Atop the seven-story hotel that was designed by Stanford White in 1906 has been added a 22-story tower with 252 guest rooms. This brings the hotel's total to 700. Utilizing the roof of the seven-story base, the architect created a roof garden with fountains and formal plantings. He also added the glass-enclosed Pavilion Room which can be seen here at the far end of the garden.

Left. Looking down on the roof garden from a room in the new tower.

Above. Four marble columns support the vaulted roof of the Pavilion Room that looks out on the seventh-floor rooftop garden. Above the dark walnut dance floor is a 24-foot diameter wrought iron chandelier finished in antique gold with imported crystals and amber prisms. Wool carpet and the gauze draperies are purple and turquoise.

Left. Despite today's higher construction costs, it was considered important that the new rooms not be skimpy in comparison with the old. The guest at the Fairmont not only has the spaciousness of a bygone era, but also the modern, comfortable furnishings and 20th Century plumbing. In this plan of typical guest rooms, the width is 15 feet compared with the usual 13 and the ceiling height is nine feet two inches compared with the normal eight feet four inches. With room-width windows offering awesome views of San Francisco, there was no compulsion to overdo the furnishings.

Over. The shaft of light on the 22-story tower of the Fairmont is the Skylift, the glass-walled elevator that takes you to the Crown Room on the roof. Offering an unopposed view of the bay area, this room is a tough competitor for the older Top of the Mark.

VI—REJUVENATING THE OBSOLETE

Given the choice of accommodations for a trip from New York to Los Angeles, would you take a seat on a forty-year-old railroad coach or a champagne flight in a jetliner? In terms of contrast, this is just about the situation in which most hotels find themselves today. What can be done with all those old hotels with their hundreds of thousands of rooms that can no longer compete? What can be done with hotels that may only be thirty-five years old, but must be considered prehistoric in terms of the jet age?

Within the industry there is growing agreement that remodeling and refurbishing pay off in higher room rates and in brisker trade at the bar and in the dining rooms. But one thing must be kept in mind by the hotel owner who is afraid of throwing good money after bad. A hotel with a reputation for mediocrity of service and operation is not going to solve its problems with remodeling. C. J. Mack, managing director of the Mayflower in Washington, says that rehabilitation of a high quality can give an older hotel the appeal to match the newest and most modern inn. But, Mack warns that a hotel without a good reputation for service when physical decay began to set in, is in a bad way. In his opinion:

> It is good management that provides a hotel with a good reputa-
> tion. No amount of paint, tile, and furnishings can completely
> wipe out a shabby past.

> A hotel is a city within a city. It is a fantastically complicated machine

More and more, as we attempt to bring out new model rooms, we are becoming gadget-conscious instead of conscious of providing our guests with clean and restful facilities.

Richard B. Ziegler
Pick Hotels Corporation

of concrete, wiring, plaster, and lumber with applied decoration; nevertheless, it is like a person. It must possess a style that comes from within. In his charming story of the Savoy in London, Compton Mackenzie wrote that from the day the hotel opened its doors in 1889, it had

> never for a moment ceased to possess a creative life of its own, and therefore one never hears it said that the Savoy is no longer the leading hotel in Europe.

THE HARDLY OBSOLETE

Our calculations on the value of remodeling are based largely on the added revenue or occupancy that such a program would produce in relation to its cost.

Ernest Henderson, President
Sheraton Corporation

I recalled that line in 1959 when Hotel Corporation of America commissioned our office to handle a four million dollar restoration of the Plaza, the magnificent dowager on Central Park in New York (see illustrations, page 150). This was no ordinary hotel calling for help. The mere fact of the refurbishings pulled one of the tweedy "Talk of the Town" reporters of *The New Yorker* magazine away from his desk (they are frightening, you know, the way they amble about, sucking on a pipe and never seeming to take a note). "The Plaza is like a lady who over the years has become more beautiful, in a way, but whose wardrobe has been neglected," I told him. "We've tried to enhance what already exists."

Where does one start on such a job? What is to be discarded? The late Barney Allis, who was veteran innkeeper at the Muehlebach in Kansas City, was often heard to grumble that the only suggestion he got from a designer was to throw out all the furniture and start all over again. "I've even had them tell me to spend $3,000 a room," he exploded during one interview. "They ought to know that's impossible because you can't earn that kind of money back." At the Muehlebach, Allis concentrated on making large rooms out of small rooms through better use of furniture to create more living space. His pet peeve was a soiled carpet. After that irritation was relieved, he moved on to the lighting and the bathrooms.

Allis was probably correct in feeling that the carpeting is of prime importance in an old hotel. The walls must be cleaned and constantly maintained. At the Plaza, much of the furniture is old-fashioned, but it is not disturbing because this is a restoration project. The hotel was being rehabilitated without making it modern. On such a job, the draperies and the upholstered furnishings demand more attention than the casegoods, the nightstands, or the headboards.

To walk into a room at the Plaza is to encounter a certain atmosphere of outmodedness and the trouble most often lies in the scale: the chests are too cumbersome and so are the chairs; the lamps are small and inadequate. This is true even in what would be termed a traditional room, for there is a difference between what we will accept as traditional and what we consider old-fashioned. Our eyes are accustomed to a different scale than that popular twenty-five years ago. In many of the rooms of the Plaza, there is a sense of clutter that makes the areas appear smaller; bits and pieces of furniture abound that are not comfortable and not even useful in some cases. As with most older hotels, the Plaza had fallen victim to a series of housekeepers who moved furniture from room to room as pieces wore out or were broken. In the restoration much of the heavy furniture was discarded, especially heavy chests with big doors and the spindle-legged desks of indistinct period.

The most popular piece of furniture in the modern hotel room is the dresser-desk, a combination of chest and work area. This can be clean and modern or designed in a traditional style appropriate for a hotel like the Plaza. Its use eliminates the need for a high chest, a low chest, and a desk. By combining these functions, the room is developed to a better sense of scale and larger living space is gained. In many instances, twin beds fit easily into rooms that had previously been sold as a double. The higher rate must certainly be considered an economic advantage of the new design.

The television set is a special problem in hotels like the Plaza. There's something so "modernistic" about that electronic Cyclops. The TV set fits easily into new hotels, but in hotels like the Plaza it produces a certain uneasiness in a room. In suites it is more easily overcome by the use of a cabinet styled to suit the rest of the furniture but in smaller rooms the TV set is hard to assimilate and rarely ever quite loses its strangeness.

There are those who contend that a hotel room should be no place like home. I feel it should be. It should be like a well-designed and well-decorated home, one of which to be proud. In the lobby and the other public spaces, monumental, exciting, and glamorous design is feasible. There is a larger scale to manipulate and these areas must appeal to different kinds of people simultaneously and in a more impersonal way.

A guestroom, on the other hand, is for intimate and comfortable use and should be of a quality to give the guest a feeling of naturalness. It must not be so over-decorated that he finds it impossible to lounge and sleep easily. This is not an invitation to make a room uninteresting. In some of the traditional rooms at the Plaza, contemporary coffee tables have been used to provide balance and interest.

In the 18th century, the best interior designers did not use contemporary styles to the exclusion of all others. They used things from the past that they felt to be good to strike a balance. Today's interior designer can do the same with the introduction of antiques in a contemporary room, or he can reverse his field and use a piece like the Mies Barcelona chair or a sparkling stainless steel table with glass or marble top to accent a room steeped in tradition. It may sound incongruous, but it works when well done.

The reporter for *The New Yorker* who covered the Plaza story asked editorially, "How many 54-year-old New Yorkers have four million dollars at their disposal simply to improve their appearance?" But on the other side of the coin, Neal Lang, the Plaza's vice president and general manager at that time, had never had the privilege of running a new hotel. "I have always wrestled with older houses like the Plaza, and this one is the most formidable and frustrating," he said.

As Lang put it, the problems of remodeling the Plaza arose from the fact that it was built for another era and was now being subjected to a change in pace and a change in time, as well as a change in the ideas of both management and guest. Yet this experienced hotel man was careful to point out that all the formidable problems of remodeling were worth challenging and were solvable because this was the Plaza, the exception that proves the rule.

There are no hard and fast rules for determining where the dollars should go in the remodeling of a hotel. Most of the older ones in downtown locations sorely need parking facilities. Commercial hotels find themselves unable to compete for the convention business because of a lack of large areas for meetings and banquets.

In the case of the Plaza, the management said, "We will spend all the money we have available to restore this hotel to its original grandeur." Which is no small challenge. When the doors opened October 1, 1907, *Architectural Record* commented that the Plaza included,

> besides sumptuous decoration, the latest devices that make for facility of operation and the maximum of comfort for the most exacting and fastidious hotel patron. Here a wealthy man can establish a permanent, attractive residence without the trouble of having to look after its maintenance; nor need he dismiss his servants when he goes abroad or to his country seat.

Fifty-five years later, the management was struggling with the problem of basement kitchens a block away from the restaurants. Waiters at the Plaza must climb two flights of stairs to reach the restaurants. The kitchens should, of course, be moved closer to the diners, but there are some remodeling jobs that are too costly to be practical. "No matter what we do, we cannot speed up food operations," said former vice president and general manager Lang. "The man in a hurry to eat must go elsewhere. You simply can't eat at the Plaza. You dine there."

The Hilton chain bought the Plaza in 1943 and several million dollars were spent on the hotel. Conrad Hilton ran into stern looks from old-time residents everytime he touched a plant or started to make the slightest change. He did manage to move a stockbroker out of one area and brought back the historic Oak Room which put him in better repute with the permanent guests. Several members of the American Institute of Interior Designers had a hand in the work done while Hilton owned the Plaza. Tom Lee, David Williams, and James S. Graham were responsible for doing over many of the suites, including the State Suite, the Venetian Suite, and the Lady Mendl Suite. It was Williams who restored the grand ballroom.

THE HOTEL CORPORATION TAKES OVER

In 1960, the hotel was purchased from Hilton for Hotel Corporation of America by their president, A. M. Sonnabend. Despite the changes of a half century and despite a cycle of designers ranging from Lady Mendl to Paul McCobb and Frank Lloyd Wright, the Plaza possessed inalienable qualities that will persist until some madness drives man to destroy this queen of Gotham. As Olga Gueft of *Interiors* so well put it,

> The Plaza's greatest assets are her familiar qualities — the splendors of rich materials, magnificent spaces, authentic mementoes of the more glamorous era which produced her.

Much of the Hotel Corporation's budget had to be assigned to airconditioning, but fortunately there were few architectural changes to eat away at the dollars available for this latest restoration. Too often in new

176

construction, the designer gets only what is left after the building is up and the mechanical equipment purchased. But in remodeling, the designer is king and this provides him with the precious opportunity for demonstrating that an interior design budget can be more exact than that which management has come to expect from architects and engineers.

Care had to be taken not to make such dramatic changes that longtime residents of the Plaza would be affronted; it was bad enough having to shift permanent guests in the renovation of the 66 rooms on the fourteenth floor. Paneling, crystal chandeliers, and marble mantles remained, as did the molding and tile in the high domed bathrooms. But along with new furniture went carpeting and vinyl flooring, new draperies and wallcoverings. The vinyl was used at entrances and in bathroom hallways of suites as accents to carpeting.

As in every remodeling program, the aim was to accentuate the positive and redesign the negative. Sonnabend's goal is to put the Plaza in such fine shape that management will be able to fill it with the kind of people who travel as individuals and not have to depend on group business except perhaps in the summer doldrums. "From October 1 through June we will be able to do capacity business and the prices will not be important," he predicted.

It would, of course, be impossible for the Plaza to add any more rooms; in any case, the management would not think it wise. In this vein, Neal Lang had said,

> We want a class operation and the more rooms you have, the greater the margin for error. With 945 rooms, of which 130 are permanently occupied, we have a chance to inject a high degree of personal service. When we get the occupancy of the Plaza up to 85 per cent, we will be able to render a type of service that no other hotel can touch. I'm talking about things like having the bellman walk through the dining room with a name on a small blackboard so we don't have to shout a page call or broadcast it; keeping a page on revolving doors so the guest doesn't have to work at enjoying the facilities.

In employee relations, the management has always attempted to instill in the staff the idea that it is a privilege to work at the Plaza. This, however, is an admittedly difficult task. Said Lang,

> With people in the mood they are today, they think of their takehome pay before they think about giving the guest better service.

THE COSTS OF REMODELING

Does remodeling pay? It does when it brings more people into the hotel and enables management to cater to them more efficiently. Robert P. Herzog, general manager of the Walter Ballard Corporation, made an excellent point in an article written for *Interior Design* magazine. He said,

> The test of our success does not lie in the pleasant comments of our fellow interior designers and the "oohs" of local society people, but rather in the hotel or restaurant's operational statements.

All too often in hotel properties, rehabilitation is a task delegated to the housekeeper, the house painter, and in many instances, the manager's wife.

J. William Keithan, General Manager Western Service & Supply Company From: Hotel Monthly

Herzog checked on 62 hotels that had recently undergone renovation programs and discovered that four out of five of them had raised rates an average of $1.87 per room and had encountered a minimum of customer complaints at paying more. As Herzog put it,

It is easier to get $10 a night for an attractive room than to collect $3 for an iron-bedded, rundown cubicle.

Of the hotels surveyed, about half had spent money to improve public spaces including dining areas, lobby, and special function rooms. Of these, three out of four reported making strong gains in sales of banquets and meetings.

The purpose of the Herzog survey was to convince management that remodeling is good business. It was also designed to give the interior designer an argument to use in selling his services. But the Ballard executive warned his fellows that they must be careful to produce a remodeling program of a practical nature. Speaking of designers, he said,

They have to know the financial intricacies of how their clients operate. They have to comprehend the problems that their clients face and they must sense public taste.

Certainly, designers must be more businesslike than is now generally the case. In the preparation of this book, letters went out to leaders in the many fields that contribute to the hotel industry. There were responses from owners, management, and architects. But, with few exceptions, letters to interior designers were met by silence. It is doubtful that this result has anything to do with the competitive nature of the business; a much more likely reason is the unbusinesslike manner so many interior designers employ in the operation of their offices. Even the simple task of replying to a letter is sloughed off. It is an attitude that bewilders the businessman-client.

But to return to Herzog's conclusions. It scarcely seems necessary that the average interior designer know how to carve his way through the financial jungle that has grown up around today's hotel industry. That is a task more suited to the contract houses which usually provide more help with money than with design anyway. There is also a danger in regarding the designer as one who is supposed to respond in a manner conforming with current public taste. Rather, the designer should be a leader of taste. If television programs are accurate reflections, as they are supposed to be, of public taste, then designers certainly should be expected to aim at a higher mark. The designer should elevate taste, but always be restrained by the fear of creating effects that the public does not understand. To do so would be folly because it would produce a basic fear and drive people away from a hotel. There must be a happy marriage of the aesthetic and the practical. Says Herzog,

The contribution of the interior designer and decorator has traditionally been minimized in the business world. We must assume our rightful role as purveyors of good taste as well as good sense. We've just grown from being artistic and perhaps a little unrealistic — we're now full-fledged business people.

THE PICK-CONGRESS

One of the biggest remodeling jobs of recent years took place at the Pick-Congress in Chicago. The Congress was built before the turn of the century, and had 1,000 rooms. By mid-century its convention facilities were proving inadequate to compete for the large organizations attracted to Chicago. Albert Pick, Jr., president of the hotel chain, found that, "The hotel's location on Michigan Avenue was getting better and the hotel was getting worse." Pick bought the hotel in 1950 and started immediately on a program to fix up the guestrooms. But by the time one third of them were refurbished, it was time to start all over again. Furthermore, the work was not solving the main problem of a lack of group business, nor was it extensive enough to overcome many of the faults that were inherent simply because of the age of the structure — such things as ancient plumbing, inadequate wiring, and ugly cast iron radiators.

In changing the program, the first big decision was to install a central air-conditioning system with individual room controls which got rid of the ugly radiators. Careful planning during the two-year project kept a minimum of seventy guestrooms out of service at any one time. With the new air-conditioning system came dividends in lower maintenance costs for walls, upholstery, and carpeting.

Holabird and Root, architects and engineers, literally remade the first three floors of the Pick-Congress to provide convention facilities. As a result there is now a new ballroom, 57 feet by 145 feet, that will handle 2,000 persons for meetings; there are more than thirty meeting rooms served by escalators and new automatic elevators that move 15,000 persons an hour.

Rebuilding the hotel was out of the question. Costs would have been out of reach and as Pick put it, "It would have killed much of the business it had already built up. How much of it could have been recaptured later was problematical. Large-scale layoffs of employees would also have been necessary."

Has the remodeling helped? In a special article published in 1961, *Hotel World-Review* reported that in 1955, before the work was done, the Pick-Congress was getting 65% of its room business from transients and 35% from conventions. After the remodeling, the figures were reversed. Banquet sales of food and liquor more than doubled with the completion of the convention facilities. *Hotel World-Review* reported that the average room rate increased from $11.63 in May, 1960, to $12.21 in May, 1961. This was the result of a $1 per day increased charge for all rooms on which remodeling had been completed.

There was some conflict among the design staff as to the styling of guestrooms. It was never resolved because design department chief Walter Thornton wound up with what he termed a compromise between period and contemporary decor. The Pick-Congress is included here, not as an example of fine restyling of interiors, but to show how a hotel seventy years old can face up to the invasion from the suburbs and highways of the motor hotels with their clean bright faces and cheerful interiors.

Pick did not, of course, stop with new public spaces. All the old plumbing fixtures were torn out and the generously sized bathrooms were completely tiled. Large mirrors and a lavatory counter replaced ancient medicine chests. Wooden window frames were replaced with weather-tight aluminum ones. The sills no longer constantly need painting since wood was replaced by sills of plastic that match the furniture and can quickly be wiped clean. In remodeling the guestrooms, the architects lowered ceilings two feet and did away with ceiling-hung fixtures that produced unflattering light. Now a switch at the door controls a floor lamp and around the baseboard is an electric strip that provides outlets every thirty inches. These outlets are linked to the switch at the door so that all lamps can be controlled either from the entrance or at the source.

It must be stressed that, as experienced hotel men have learned, a superficial facelifting is not enough to bring back lost customers.

HOTEL NEW ORLEANS

The Hotel New Orleans (see illustrations, page 156) is an example of a job that was not thorough enough. The architectural firm of Curtis and Davis came up with an exceedingly fine design to change the face of the hotel. The basic economics of room occupancy were not changed because practically all the money was spent on the lobby and public spaces and nothing on the guestrooms. The latter, after the remodeling was completed, still looked like 1910 and in one room at least, a naked fluorescent fixture is the only light. Yet from the street, the Hotel New Orleans is an exciting image. Front and side are covered with a brick veneer to a height of 32 feet and dramatically lighted. Even the newsstand at the curb has been glamorized with plastic to look like a handsome sideboard.

Lobby floors are covered with terrazzo and wall surfaces have been transformed by gleaming white plastic panels accented with vertical strips in red. Individual furniture pieces in the lobby are all prize winners: a Knoll sofa in leather, Mies Van der Rohe Barcelona chairs, and George Nelson's Marshmallow sofa and cocoanut chairs. After these handsome and dramatic spaces it is too great a shock for the guest walking into a bedroom of a bygone era.

We can automate the Plaza extensively behind the scenes, but out front at the guest level we must never do anything that would mean a loss in personal service.

Neal Lang
Hotel Manager

One of the golden rules in hotel interior designing is to spend the money where it will show. This aphorism is matched by the one that the guest must first be provided with what he came for: a comfortable bed in a pleasant room. One step without the other is well-nigh useless.

In the view of Sam Revness, the president of the Ballard Corporation, a careful appraisal must be made for each hotel for which a remodeling or refurbishing of interiors is being considered and the appraisal must take into account the type of client wanted. He added,

> Every new hotel that goes up throws into obsolescence a half dozen old ones. These then must improve or get out of business. But since you can't turn every hotel into an office building with butcher shops and shoe stores on the ground floor, the fact of obsolescence must be faced.

Revness puts most of the blame for declining occupancy in older hotels on management that has failed to recognize its own shortcomings.

180

The owners of the marginal hotels haven't been on the ball. They haven't looked at their own operation closely enough to see where the fault really lies. Now they are being forced to get abreast of the times by the new motels coming into metropolitan areas.

Blunt, perhaps, but undoubtedly true. Bad management, more often than not, does not even recognize how shabby its hotel has become in service and appearance.

It should be noted that the Hotel New Orleans is owned by Seymour Weiss whose Roosevelt Hotel in the same city has for three years been busy with refurbishing the 413 rooms in the older section of the Roosevelt, making these rooms fresher than those added in the wing that went up in 1955. Walls were replastered and modern lighting replaced the old ceiling fixtures. According to the *Journal of American Innkeeping,*

> Murals above the bed headboards are in an oriental accented floral design. Furniture, custom designed to fit existing wall space, includes an effective and efficient dresser-desk-TV unit. The furniture is trimmed in gold anodized aluminum and has brass hardware.

All of which is fine although it is perhaps a pity that so little of what was done has any relation to the tradition and elegance of the city.

Compare it with what was achieved for the Prince Conti Motor Hotel in the heart of the New Orleans French Quarter (see illustrations, page 154). Under the direction of architect Eugene Gilbert and interior designer Charles Gresham, a former coffin factory was transformed into one of the most charming places in the Quarter. Built anywhere else but where it is, the Prince Conti would be pretentious. But its charm is exactly suited to its environment and it offers the tourist the very whimsy and elegance he is seeking when he marks his road map for a trip to New Orleans.

The exterior of the former factory (later a warehouse) is old brick with a band of the familiar iron balconies stretched across the arched windows. Here are none of those obscenely large blinking neon signs with flashing arrows that so often provide the motorist with his first impression of a motor hotel. The Prince Conti has copper lanterns and a coral and white awning over the carriageway leading to a patio and continuing on into the parking area. This patio is in the tradition of the courtyard that was the heart of the early English inns. From here the guest can walk into the lobby or into a cocktail lounge called Le Petit Bar.

All the bedrooms are furnished with antiques and consequently no two are alike. A liberal use of four poster beds creates the feeling of romanticism suitable in a city like New Orleans. Most of the bedrooms are small but, whenever possible, the designer has used large pieces such as a massive carved headboard or provincial armoire.

The lobby of the Prince Conti is also small, but was not intended to serve as a general meeting place. Visitors to New Orleans are not lobby sitters. Here the lobby has the atmosphere of an 18th century drawing room with putty-colored, damask-covered walls and antique furnishings.

This must be classed as a major success in the collaboration of architecture and design. It is a job that has won the praise of the profession

The selection of a professional rehabilitation specialist is not often easy. Many hold themselves out to be such, but not often is this the fact of the matter. Sometimes an answering service and a sports car make impression enough to represent one as a qualified designer.

J. William Keithan, General Manager
Western Service & Supply Company
From: Hotel Monthly

It is not what the interior looks like on completion — but how it looks years later — that really matters. Whether the interior in question is a two-room apartment or a 1000-bed hotel, he has specified the materials to be used. He must be aware of their advantages and disadvantages: how long they will last and how they should be cared for, and who will be responsible for their maintenance and what methods will be used.

Bodil W. Nielsen
Interiors

but, just as important, it has been enthusiastically accepted by the people who check in at the front desk.

SHERATON TOWERS

No two hotels are alike in their remodeling problems. The Pick-Congress in Chicago had a lot of old rooms, but simply bringing them up to date would not have solved the problem of the lack of convention facilities. Further up Michigan Boulevard, the Sheraton Towers (see illustrations, page 158) was at the other end of the spectrum. It had fine areas for meeting and banquets, but only 500 rooms — not enough to bring in the major trade associations that look to Chicago as a strategic city for conventions.

While the Sheraton was in good physical shape, it did not have those extra touches of luxury which attract today's sophisticated businessman. The answer was a ten million dollar addition of 600 finely appointed guestrooms and a new entrance connecting this wing to the old one.

To meet the competition of the motor hotels springing up in downtown Chicago, Sheraton provided a drive-in entrance with parking and its own registration desk. The guest coming in from a day of turnpike driving can go straight to his rooms without having to struggle with an old-fashioned lobby. The exterior of the 42-story tower was steam cleaned to match the freshness of its 25-story younger brother and the interiors were redecorated and brought up to the standards of the new wing. The Sheraton design staff was given a generous budget and the guestrooms represent a high standard for hotel accommodations.

Elliott Mizelle, while manager of the Ambassador Hotel in Los Angeles, stressed the importance of the guestrooms in remodeling programs.

> I would say that the propitious thing is to put all sleeping accommodations in the best possible order. In older hotels, much of your budget must necessarily be placed in the modernization of the plumbing, without which all decoration and rehabilitation is useless.

Mizelle, a native of Australia, has had world-wide hotel experience. He worked in Paris and London and he was the manager of the Ambassador in Chicago before joining the Schine organization on the West Coast. If he had any money left after putting the guestrooms in top condition, Mizelle would turn to the approach to the hotel, an area he calls one of the most neglected in hotels everywhere. He mentioned the pavement outside the entrance, one of those factors that is rarely considered when management, architect, and designer sit down to discuss a new image for a hotel. Mizelle was always careful about the shrubbery and flowers at the Ambassador. "Once all of these are in shape, then I would move into the lobby and public spaces," he stated.

In Washington, the general manager of the Mayflower, Neal Mack, said the opposite. His hotel is 35 years old and work on it is constant. But he puts the emphasis on the lower lobby and the public spaces. This is logical since the Mayflower is the center of political and diplomatic social

I dreamed that Congress passed a bill to provide that older hotels which would agree to be plowed under into a parking lot or a senior citizens' residence would be paid a subsidy to compensate the owners for not operating them.

*Allen C. George
Harris, Kerr, Forster & Company*

activity and the public spaces are vital because of the many banquets and receptions held in the hotel. The hotel is superbly equipped to handle the most lavish of functions. After the Soviet Union gave a reception at the Mayflower for President Dwight Eisenhower, representatives of the Russian Government approached Mack and asked about buying the silver and the gold plate. The answer was no.

COCOANUT GROVE

One of the most extensive jobs undertaken at the forty-year-old Ambassador in Los Angeles was the redecoration of the famous Cocoanut Grove (see illustrations, page 155). Back in the dim days of radio, all of America tuned in on the orchestras that played for dancing under the palms that gave the room its name and character.

As design consultant for Schine Hotel Corporation, I was given the task of refurbishing the Grove and restoring its rich atmosphere. It seemed apparent that what was needed here was an atmospheric quality largely dependent on sensual effects created by light and shade. In short, it had to have the magical and dramatic qualities of a theater setting.

Tom Lee, A.I.D., whose work included settings for the musical, *Louisiana Purchase,* agreed to act as design associate for the Cocoanut Grove. We both believed that the original concept of the room was not to be sacrificed just to give the place a fresh look. Good decoration in large areas like this one is usually a part of the very structure of the building and regardless of one's opinion of the original design, the nature of the rooms could not be changed. This settled, the job became one of retaining the good and eliminating the gingerbread to simplify the details. The original Moorish style was emphasized with a striking archway silhouetting the entrance. Large white screens with an open grillework in Moorish tile design were used on each side of the entrance arch and also as a backdrop for the bandstand. The same style was used in the lighting fixtures strung from the ceiling and for the table lights.

Because so much of the Grove's atmosphere depends on dramatic lighting, about one-fifth of the $500,000 budget was assigned to it. Hundreds of fixtures were recessed into the ceiling. This was not simply to provide a starry effect at night, but to make the room bright for daytime sessions of conventions and for banquets and fashion shows when more brilliance than atmosphere is desired. Cantilevered into the room and incorporated in the overall design is a control room for an elaborate lighting system. It is much like those used in theaters so that the individual areas of the room can be lighted with any desired intensity or color.

There is always a best way of doing everything, if it be to boil an egg. Manners are the happy ways of doing things.

Ralph Waldo Emerson
1803-1882

The palms must not be forgotten. There is truly a grove of them standing twenty feet tall with gilded fronds reflecting simulated moonlight.

THE PIERRE

The theatrical concept was also utilized in the remodeling of the ballroom of the Pierre Hotel in New York. The architect, Henry J. Stojowski, worked in conjunction with lighting specialist Leslie Wheel and with Alice

Jenner who is in charge of the hotel's modernization program. The goal was a room capable of handling everything from a small private reception to an automobile show. Flexibility of spaces was a must and it was worked out with a system of folding walls. These have acoustic filling and are faced with laminated vinyl in a wood tone. The architect achieved the goal with ten divisions of space and avoided traffic snarls for waiters on their appointed rounds with drink and food. The hotel can feed as many as 300 persons in two bays of the room and have a large area left over for pre-dining cocktails or a reception.

The lighting not only provides theatrical effects, but is used to bypass some of the architectural weightiness of the room; a luminous soffit magically makes the beams between bays disappear. There is a central lighting control board in the control booth, but also available are three smaller units that can be operated by the waiters to change the mood of smaller areas within the ballroom.

BROADMOOR HOTEL

Preserving the best of the past was an approach also taken with the Broadmoor Hotel, Colorado Springs (see illustrations, page 162), which had been built in 1918. Some brief thought was given to using a western theme, but Leslie Dorsey of W. & J. Sloane's contract division quickly changed his mind because the Broadmoor was so "very continental and European looking."

What he did was capture the elegance of a bygone era, brush it up and advance it. It is lavish, yes, but tasteful. A forty-year collection of art objects and paintings became the theme of the refurbishing program. In the grand corridor to the ballroom, rich furnishings were used to set off the original arched and painted ceiling. It would have been a serious mistake not to have put this emphasis on the architectural grandeur of the past. Everything Dorsey did was aimed at enhancing ornamentation of 1918 and at the same time blending in the comfort and glamour of modern furnishings and accessories.

NEW WESTON HOTEL

The Broadmoor, primarily a resort hotel, had an English feeling that also exists in the New Weston in midtown Manhattan. It has long been a favorite of the continental visitor to the United States and for good reason: every afternoon there is high tea in the cocktail lounge.

Knott Hotel Corporation spent 18 months on a rehabilitation program that provided air-conditioning and a thorough renovation of the guestrooms. Leon Heygood, A.I.D., of the Dorothy Draper Company, introduced color to the New Weston: brilliant reds in draperies, bedding, and carpeting; new furniture includes black teak with brass fittings; even the bathrooms have taken on color with flowered wall coverings that are washable.

Knott has combined the comfortable feeling of an English country home with modern American plumbing, heating, and service. The 90% occupancy rate proves the wisdom of the investment.

KENILWORTH

Extensive remodeling is not always necessary in older hotels; sometimes a simple refurbishing program is sufficient. A case in point is the Kenilworth in Bal Harbour (see illustrations, page 164), just north of hotel row in Miami Beach, which refused to join the race for new business through package deals for conventions.

New ownership, which includes Arthur Godfrey and Washington attorney Leo D'Orsey, left the management to Edwin O. Kirkeby, member of a family experienced in the hotel business. While all around him hotels were downgrading to meet competition, Kirkeby decided to try the opposite tack. First came a complete refurbishing of the public areas. The lobby was made formal with low furniture to contrast with the heavy marble-faced columns that march symmetrically toward the ocean from the entrance. Dining areas have become brighter and more cheerful; furniture is lighter in scale. This was a particularly satisfying job because the Kenilworth Hotel had never, in the past, done very well. The management realized, too, that to achieve the degree of luxury they desired it would be necessary to spend a good deal of money. As a result, they allowed a generous budget for the remodeling.

QUEENSBURY HOTEL

The situation was the reverse in the refurbishing of the forty-year-old Queensbury Hotel in Glens Falls, N. Y. At the Kenilworth, the clientele is rich and conservative. So is the city of Glens Falls. But the Schine management recognized that the Queensbury could never increase rates enough to pay for costly remodeling.

Much of the original furniture which was dull and drab was salvaged by reupholstery. However, draperies for the lobby and dining room were in the budget and fabrics were used to contrast with the highly decorative columns and moldings of the ceilings. Since no architectural changes were planned in the lobby, subdued colors were used to match the look of age. In the suites, for which the budget allowed good contemporary furnishings, the colors are more lively with touches of Siamese red and pink.

HOTEL SHERMAN

Just as some of the older hotels are building specialty restaurants to keep their guests from spending money off the premises, so are they adding suites big enough to provide luxurious living quarters and separate business conference areas for executives who are accustomed to the best. The Hotel Sherman (see illustrations, page 160) redesigned a penthouse that combines the comforts of a private home with the convenience of hotel living. Everett Brown Associates paneled the drawing room with black walnut and used a French petit point rug. The draperies are gold velveteen. This demonstration of great taste and ability on the part of the designer provides the Sherman with an excellent showplace.

HOTEL NAVARRO

A desire for utmost luxury prompted a rejuvenation of the Hotel Navarro in New York (see illustrations, page 168). International Hotels,

A hotel designer should spend most of the budget where it will show because you can achieve a very handsome and comfortable effect in guest rooms without spending a great deal of money. On the other hand, it is difficult to make a budget job in public spaces come off well because you have such factors as high ceilings and architectural effects that demand more of you.

Emily Malino, A.I.D.

Inc., of Detroit bought the hotel in 1956, recognizing its prime location on Central Park South and its potential "to produce the ultimate in luxury living."

The lobby presented problems typical of most older hotels. It was a miserable dark green with a clutter of beams, pilasters, and wainscoating. The lighting was old and quite hopeless. The solution was to drop the ceiling and then highlight it with a grandiose chandelier. Walls were smoothed out. An antique mirror gave the small area a sense of larger dimensions.

Upstairs, the first task was the rejuvenation of the one and two bedroom suites whose generous size and serving pantries had long attracted both corporate and individual guests on a permanent basis. But time had taken its toll of the furnishings: not shabby, really, but dated. Because of the ample space in the suites, it was not necessary to set a formula for the furnishings. Each suite could have a character of its own. There was space for art work and large-scale accessories. Areas for relaxation and entertaining were easily found, and all without architectural changes of major note.

From the suites, the luxurious restyling was carried over into the smaller transient guestrooms. The demand for the single rooms, with their rich decor, was so much greater than had been anticipated that some replanning became essential.

The Navarro is a comparative newcomer to the New York hotel scene, but its management recognized the need for change to meet the challenge of the modern marketplace.

As shown clearly in the survey by Walter Ballard Corporation, every example of professional management combined with experienced interior design has proved that the public wants and will patronize hotels whose facilities are modern and attractive. The investments in professional refurbishing have resulted in higher rates and higher occupancy.

VII – PROCEDURES

Illustrations

The text for this Chapter will be found on pages 197 to 217

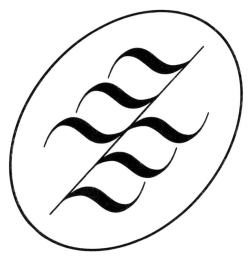

GRAPHICS

The graphics program is an important aspect of hotel design. Through it the hotel can establish an identity and aura which can effect its stature around the world. A symbol has frequently come to speak volumes for the concern it represents. In the case of the Denver Hilton, a complete graphics program was worked out while the hotel was still under the auspices of William Zeckendorf. The hotel changed hands and this particular program was only partially used — the logo and name were dropped but the general lettering plans were retained. However, the original program illustrates so well the approach desirable that it is worth examination. To the left is the logo to have been used as a symbol throughout the hotel and above is shown its use on various bathroom items.

On the facing page the Zeckendorf name is used on towels along with the symbol, the latter being carried through on telephone directory, notebook, and ashtray.

Graphics program by Page Graphics

GRAPHICS

A graphics program necessarily includes lettering. In this case it was designed for use in a variety of places and carried through in a recognizably consistent fashion.

See page 215 for further graphics.

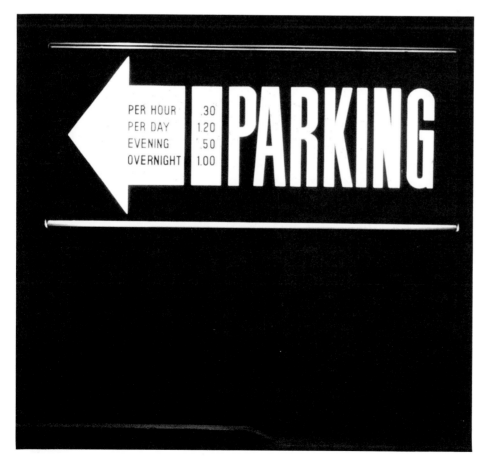

On this and the following two pages are examples of floor plans which show layout solutions to a variety of spaces.

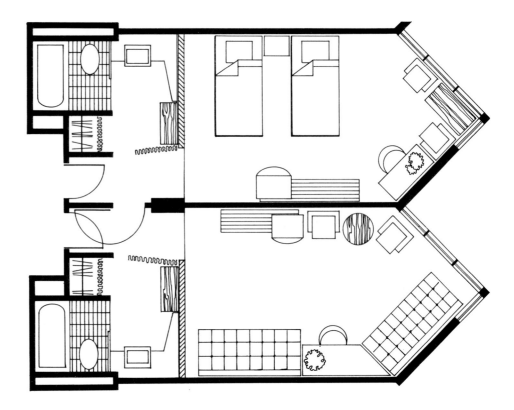

**RIVERVIEW MOTOR HOTEL,
NEW YORK, N. Y.**

Two possible layouts for the same space. At
the top is a fairly conventional twin-bed arrangement; below, beds are convertible to sofas
for daytime use and for greater spaciousness.
Closets are placed in the compact bathroom
area — the only moot point in this layout since
their size is not overgenerous and their accessi-
bility might be a problem. The rooms can be
combined for suite accommodation.

**AMERICANA OF PUERTO
RICO, SAN JUAN,
PUERTO RICO**

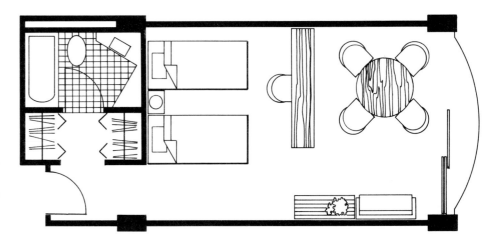

This is a typical layout for this hotel which provides living, sleeping, and generous bathroom
areas for its guests. Foyer, closet area, and bathroom form one spatial unit, bedroom the next,
and living area the third. Sliding doors lead
onto a curved balcony.

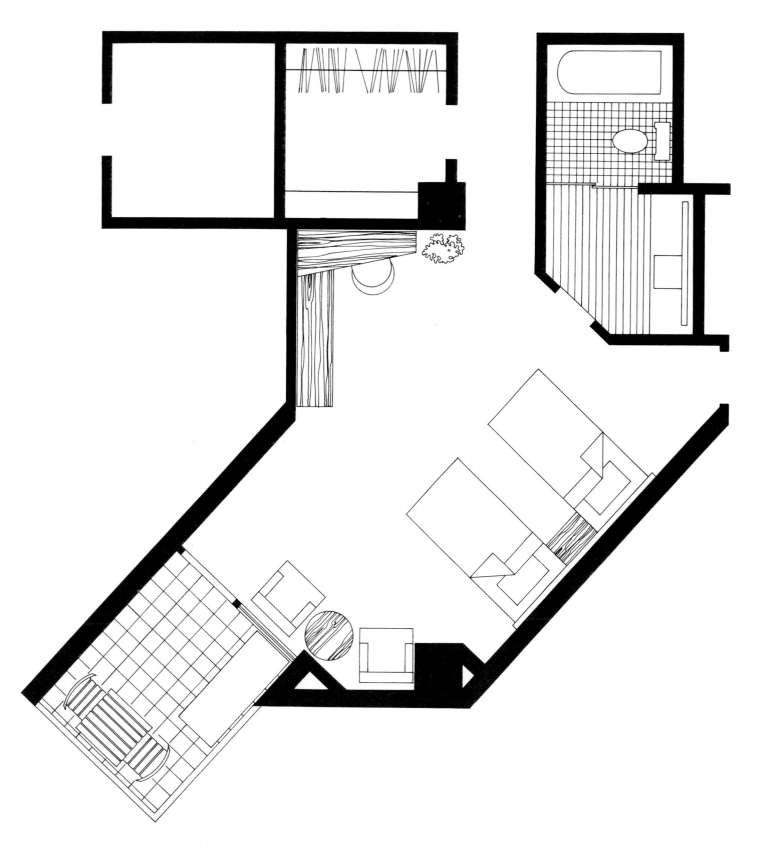

**ARUBA CARIBBEAN,
WILLEMSTAD,
NETHERLANDS ANTILLES**

Simply furnished and generously spaced, this
room at the Aruba Caribbean provides generous
closet space for guests with piles of holiday
clothing, plus a glass-enclosed loggia for con-
templation of the sun-baked view.

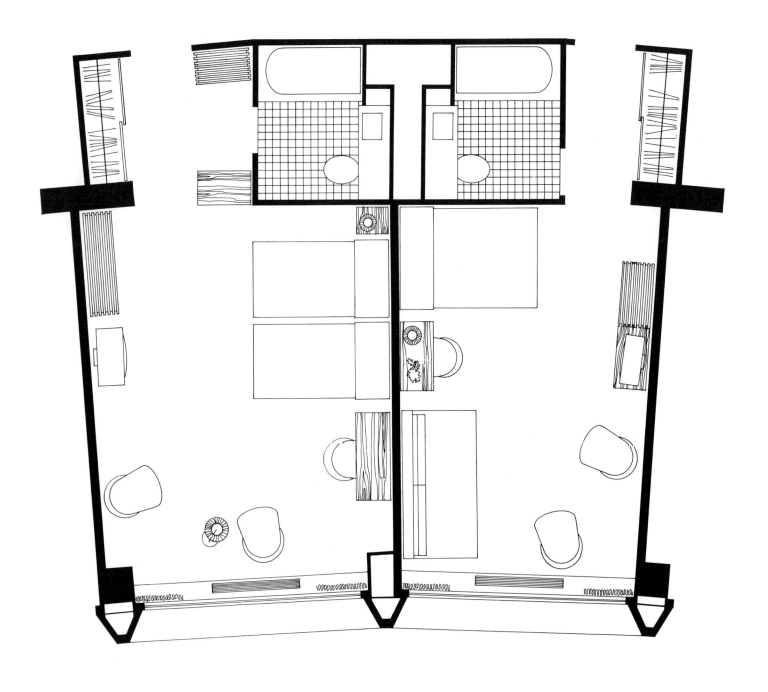

**WASHINGTON HILTON,
WASHINGTON, D. C.**

This new hotel by the Hilton organization (see page 223 for exterior view) will cater to many diplomat guests and other visitors to the nation's capital. Guest accommodations have been designed accordingly; here are two layouts of slightly differing spaces. In the larger one to the left twin beds are left undisguised and the generous space is relied upon for comfortable living quarters. To the right a double bedroom is shown with the large sofa available for a third (and even fourth) member of the party. Since the bed is tucked into a corner, more space is available for living quarters in spite of the actually smaller area.

VII—PROCEDURES

When the National Hotel opened in Washington in 1827, the National Intelligencer commented that hotels had become "palaces of the people."

The world of luxurious living, once the monopoly of the landed gentry in their country estates and the industrial tycoons in their mansions, was now available to anyone with the price of a night's lodging in his pocket.

The hotel is still one of the most exciting creations of American capitalism; "a thermometer and barometer of our national civilization," one writer called it many years ago. But the hotel is also a creation of major capital investments. The first real one in New York was built by a stock company. The latest grand hotel in New York, San Francisco, or London is reflected in daily quotations on the major stock exchanges.

By any standard, hotel design is difficult.

Stephen Garrett
Design

So while the hotel offers the most exciting prospects for the interior designer, he must recognize that he is dealing with gilt-edged clients who expect and will demand a businesslike approach, manner, and performance. Although he is in an artistic profession and is given a certain amount of latitude, the designer must never adopt a capricious attitude with the hotel investor or the builder. That sort of conduct may be considered charming by the housewife or society matron redoing her bedroom, but the hotel management firm will quickly get rid of the interior designer who cannot match the architect, engineer, and builder in efficiency and the business of meeting deadlines. This applies particularly to the matter of forms and correspondence. Nothing impresses a businessman more than a speedy response with a letter that supplies the requested information. The real estate brokers do it. The interior designers must be prepared to operate no less efficiently. But in 1962, only four of the twelve major design schools in the United States offered business courses.

WHITHER SEEK YE INTERIOR DESIGNER

Speaking at an International Design Congress held in London, Emmanuel Gran stressed the point that a hotel is one of the most complex of buildings and that a great number of specialists and designers from every field must work together to achieve a well-designed hotel. Gran, the director of architecture and design for Hilton International, had this to say:

> Let us discard the idea that a hotel is a "home away from home." A hotel is a hotel and the problem of design should be approached only from this point of view. A home is designed for an individual. It develops and grows around his or her (mostly her) personality. It is designed specifically for their manner of living, their recreation, their hobbies. In contrast, a hotel caters to thousands of unknown persons of different nationalities, backgrounds, and a variety of taste. The whole structure, the interiors, everything that goes into it must possess an air of dignity, a certain character, identity with a location, presence, sense of importance, an elegance with pomposity. A hotel must offer dignified comfort and the right atmosphere. It must have the restrained sense of a stage setting and yet, above all, it must possess real warmth. From experience, we know we cannot sell a cold-looking room no matter how clean the design may be, no matter how expensively or expertly it is done.

But the selection of a designer for a hotel is a complicated and sensitive business that is afflicted with social, political, and sometimes international undertones. Where does the inexperienced hotel developer turn if he wants to assure himself of a chance at success, if he can ignore the special interest pleadings of relatives, friends, and the fellows down at the lodge?

The best solution lies in the recommendations of trade journalists. A good place to begin would be a list of ten names supplied by the editors of the top design magazines. They certainly would give no fewer than that number. The hotel man should then investigate and review the work of those so recommended. Requesting such a list from the American Hotel Association would not produce the same results. This is a dedicated and professional organization, but its executive staff could not do other than offer the names of all associate members in the design and furnishings field. The hotel trade magazines would certainly be familiar with those designers doing the more important work, though not necessarily with the best aesthetically.

A word of caution to the hotel man who had decided to take the risk of employing an inexperienced designer. If the hotel is to be done in a traditional manner, it is quite possible that the results will be reasonably acceptable to the public solely on the basis of familiarity. But beware of the neophyte attempting to accomplish the unknown in a contemporary style. He is likely to fall victim to fads and wind up with a hotel that will be gimmicky and out-of-date before the first guests register.

Igor Stravinsky said much the same thing in reflecting on recordings of contemporary music. In an article in *Hi Fi/Stereo Review*, the composer commented that

Few clients have any basis of logic for the style of building or interiors which they want, rather their tastes are based on their emotional and psychological backgrounds.

Brock Arms, AIA, NSID,
President of Interior Space Design,
Division of Perkins & Will,
Chicago Architects
From: Institutions

fifty recordings of Beethoven are fifty different angles of distortion (but that) recording of the contemporary, on the other hand, lacks comparison and therefore fixes the music at a single angle. Moreover, the greatest danger of this fixed angle is not obvious. It is that the truly contemporary must always exist on the precarious edge of the comprehensible for most people . . . . The performance of the unfamiliar is a greater responsibility and must seek higher standards than the performance of the familiar.

This becomes more and more true in the design field as the influence of American hotels becomes stronger overseas. The standards of comfort, maintenance, and mechanics have been established in the United States. When he tries to copy blindly, the inexperienced designer runs into trouble. New hotels overseas certainly reflect American designs. But there is nothing so painful as the result of a provincial approach to American techniques and experience.

What is this "professional approach" we speak of? It is the combination of professional hotel and motor hotel operators working with professional specialists.

J. William Keithan, General Manager Western Service & Supply Company From: Hotel Monthly

THE INTERIOR DESIGNER AND THE ARCHITECT

With such a wealth of experience and the benefits of technological and electronic age, it would seem a simple matter for management, architect, and designer to come up with a superlative result on every hotel project. But there still exists within the industry a shortage of communications and an oversupply of misunderstanding and distrust. It is easy to appreciate an architect's fears when he sees an interior designer brought into a program. There have been too many examples of architects being treated badly by designers who have neither training nor proper experience. The architect who creates a contemporary building is fearful that some decorator will come along and make the interiors early American.

But the good interior designer should have no trouble establishing rapport with an architect. There must be mutual respect. The architect is trained in the art of delineating ideas. He becomes impatient with the designer who is working with fabrics and colors and finishes, utilizing talents that often are nebulous. More often than not, the trouble stems from a lack of communication. The designer knows exactly what he intends to accomplish, but he cannot relate ideas easily. His sketches are often too dreamlike and out of scale.

There is no easy solution to the problem of the architect who is jealous of the interior designer's increasingly important role in the business of building new hotels and renovating old ones. Sam Revness, president of Walter Ballard Company, has suggested that the designer tell the architect immediately that there is to be no attempt to usurp his rights. Says Revness,

The designer should demonstrate that he can be very practical in supplying the architect with essential information on what will be needed later on for the interiors. The architect should not stalk off the job when it is pointed out to him where electric outlets will be needed in the lobby or the restaurant.

That is all very well, but so many architects think of themselves as creators of total design and the average architect feels he has a sense of interior design. The interior and the exterior blend together in his mind's eye and he feels only he can carry out the grand concept. But the thing that appears to irritate the architect most actually concerns the fees paid to the interior designer. It is a touchy subject and one rarely brought out into the open. Yet it is because of this "speak no evil" attitude that interior designers have created a bad public image.

One brave architect brought up the subject at a contract market seminar held at New York's National Design Center. He was David Eggers, a partner in the firm of Eggers and Higgins, vice president of the New York chapter of the American Institute of Architects and a member of the executive committee of the Architectural League of New York. Said Eggers,

> Professional ethics do not permit the architect to accept any reimbursement, direct or indirect, for the purchase of a specified product. An architect is bound to return the difference between the discount and list price to the owner. By contrast, some interior decorators and designers ask a minimal charge for their professional services, relying on trade discounts for their fee. . . . The architect may base his fee on a stipulated percentage of the cost of furnishings or he may, as we do in our firm, charge an hourly rate for professional services. I believe that both of these two arrangements are straightforward and equitable to all parties. Quite frankly, I cannot say the same for the informal agreements under which some interior decorators and designers operate, agreements which, by their very nature, can spawn questionable practices.

Eggers claimed for his profession that where architects had secured the interiors work it was to the financial benefit of the owners and said:

> I am aware that this has created friction, even to the point where it has been forcibly stated that the architect should stay out of the decorating field. I think it's high time that merchandising practices in the decorating field depart from the discount house concept. Let's stop the fancy footwork on price quotations and establish prices that allow the designer and owner to know where they stand.

This cannot be dismissed as the gripe of one architect. A.I.D. Executive Director William Hamilton was quoted in *Interiors* as saying,

> Unfortunately, the Elsie de Wolfe school — charging what you can get — is a cloud that lingers three decades later.

Priscilla Ginsberg, managing editor of the magazine, in discussing the various ways designers charge for their services, commented, "Small wonder a client approaches her decorator as if he were a rug merchant in a Turkish bazaar."

In her thoroughly provocative article, Miss Ginsberg recalled that in 1940 interior decorators were classed in the United States Census with embalmers and chorus girls. A decade later, they had managed to move up with authors and be termed professionals. The editorial pointed out that it was not until the decade of the 1950s that

> the more knowledgeable clients have begun to know what a designer can do for them; that he is selling his special knowledge of lighting, space division, traffic flow, and acoustics, and not pushing around rubber plants and peddling furniture.

This has always been one of the sore points, the fear of the client that he has fallen into the hands of an expensive middleman. Maurice Morgelescu, president of Designs for Business, urged that designers earn their fees by selling themselves as advisors.

> The important thing, and the integrity of the profession depends on it, is to get away from the reputation that a decorator is primarily interested in selling furniture at a profit.

It is the viewpoint of designer Barbara Dorn that there be a contract that specifies "labor times three." There is one-third for overhead, one-third for labor and a third for profit. She has always charged on a time basis and does not believe in the practice of speculative sketches. Miss Dorn prefers to have the client look at work by the designers they are considering and then select the one they like the best.

Another viewpoint within the profession is that room count should determine the designer's fee. Emily Malino says, "The more rooms you have and the more extensive the public spaces, the lower my percentage." She is a strong supporter of the theory that the only way to achieve a good relationship with the architect is to start working with him at the outset of the job, rather than be called in later as a play doctor would be in the case of a faltering show destined for Broadway.

It is easy to understand that a designer's fee must be based on the size of the job, but how small a project can a designer afford to take? Revness says the trouble with most hotel clients is that they fail to understand the designer goes through the same motions on a 50-room motel as he does on a 200-room hotel. Yet there must be an accepted pattern for fees. Consider a 100-room hotel. The fee for the designer should be ten per cent of the cost of furnishing the guestrooms and fifteen per cent of what it takes to complete the public areas. A logical budget would be $1,000 for each of the guestrooms and $50,000 for the public space. The designer's fee would thus be a total of $17,500.

If the hotel is in another city, it is quite normal for the client to pay travel expenses and out-of-pocket expenses, but not necessarily a set amount per day. It would apply for the designer and any of his assistants. These expenses usually cover hotel room and meals while away from the home office. If the designer is required to visit plants in Grand Rapids or North Carolina for furniture selection, expenses in most cases would be paid by the client. But a designer working on several projects at the same time would be wise to consider such a shopping trip his own business expense and not bill any of his clients for it.

Hotel owners don't understand that you go through the same gestures and motions and headaches on a 50-room motel that you do on a 200-room hotel.

Sam Revness, President
Walter Ballard Corp.

On a 300-room hotel, there is virtually the same amount of work as that involved with one a third that size. The public spaces might possibly be a little larger. But a larger dining room, a larger coffee shop, or a larger lobby does not make the task any more difficult. On the contrary, it is often more difficult to design a small space and do it well. In larger areas, the designer has more latitude. For this theoretical 300-room hotel, a fee schedule for the designer of ten per cent in the guestrooms and fifteen per cent in the public spaces would not apply. It is probable that in a job of this size, a fair fee would be seven per cent of the total sum expended. This would include sketches and renderings by the designer, plus elevations and detailing of special areas. There will probably be much shaking of heads by those who have never been involved with hotel work. The client who has dealt only with furniture supply houses might find my fee estimates outrageous. But in dealing with contract houses, the client must realize that while the services of design are advertised as free, they must certainly be included in the mark-up on the furniture and accessories.

THE ROLE OF THE INTERIOR DESIGNER

It must be stressed that the present role of the interior designer is far different from that of a few years ago. It is no longer simply that of a furniture selector. Today the interior designer should be recognized as a specialist in the architecture of interiors, who is responsible for complete planning, from the detail of wood paneling to the actual design of specific furniture and accessories for both guestrooms and public spaces.

The work of the interior designer has been made easier because more and more so-called contract furniture items are available. Yet herein lies a paradox. While he can find good contract furniture in stock styles, the interior designer has a responsibility to the client to create individual touches that make his hotel different from the one down the street.

The reader will thus begin to realize that the interior designer's fee, which may seem high to those clients whose only experience has been with the decorating departments of furniture supply houses and department stores, is economically justified. Not that those services cannot be good. Many companies throughout the country provide an excellent service. They are dedicated to supplying not only quality furniture, but good design service as well. But, these services only appear to be furnished free. Economics demands that they be included in the cost of doing business.

What is the contract business? One definition comes from Paul Bischoff, general manager of the contract division for Carson-Pirie-Scott and Company of Chicago. He calls it

> volume sales of interior furnishings and allied equipment and supplies to the non-residential consumer.

That covers a broad field and as Bischoff told a contract market seminar at the National Design Center, "It would appear at times from the competition that just about anyone with a telephone and a pogo stick to elude creditors is in the contract business."

In outlining the types of organizations selling to the contract consumer, Bischoff saved what he considered the best for last — the contract specialist

who performs best for the consumer since his services combine both design and merchandising. The two services, functioning together, offer the most economical and successful solution to any project.

He added that the department store contract division is the "agency best suited for this work through background and experience."

Before coming to grips with Bischoff's point of view, it would be best to run through the other five on his list of contract agencies. First there is the local retail furniture store. Says Bischoff,

He gets into the picture through local friendships and usually rues the day. It is interesting to note though that 33 per cent of motel furniture is purchased through the same retail dealer.

Second is the manufacturer who sells direct. Bischoff offers two choices: one is the large company that deals directly but goes through the motions of a billing through a local furniture outlet with a dictated profit margin so low that servicing would be impossible; the other is the marginal manufacturer who has no general acceptance for his product and cannot even find a local firm to front for the sale. Bischoff wisely warns that such an outfit is

often under-capitalized and a real hazard to the contract consumer. Not only will services be non-existent, but product guarantees may be useless.

The third source for the consumer is the trade supply house covering in a package deal everything from cups and saucers to towels, fabrics, carpeting, plus furniture.

Fourth is the office furniture house which Bischoff says does a good job when there are staff designers for large office installations.

The fifth is the independent designer or design firm of whom Bischoff says:

Though he does not merchandise, he is an important factor in the contract picture, being the arbiter of taste and planning.

Of his own operation, the department store executive told the design seminar,

Design is the most important service we can offer the contract consumer. Every successful undertaking must start from a plan. Since interiors are primarily used by people, human engineering must be considered first. Then aesthetics must be introduced to make the space palatable.

While design is the greatest service to be offered a client, no one can argue that there are not considerable expenses involved with the warehousing and advertising required by a large department store or furniture house. Possibly the greatest advantage of the independent interior designer is that he is dedicated solely to working out and programming the design and plans. If the designer becomes involved in merchandising and buying, he is forced to push the furniture he has on the floor and stacked up in the warehouse. By necessity and by competition, he is practically forced to align himself with certain manufacturers. As an independent, however, he has only his office and design costs just as architects do. Certainly an architect who behaves professionally and ethically does not concern himself with selling building materials, but only with the design of the structure. Nor is the price differential a vital factor: the independent designer working on a hotel project can get as good a price on 200 beds or 200 lamps or 400 chairs as a department store. The interior designer working in the hotel field is really a bulk buyer and will often place greater dollar volume orders than some furniture stores with contract divisions.

The independent designer dealing in large orders is able to modify stock designs or arrange the manufacture of original designs. The large hotel chains that maintain their own design staffs will not accept whatever the manufacturers happen to be pushing this year. Joseph R. Haddock, president of Sheraton's Standard Wholesale Supply Corporation, said it this way: "Buying is so tied in with design that it is hard to talk about one without mentioning the other." With a strong design department, buyers for Sheraton have learned they are wasting their time talking with manufacturers whose products are not first-rate aesthetically. At the same time, the hotel staff designers know high style will not carry the day if the buyers are not completely satisfied as to price and quality.

Haddock is also head of International Hotel Supply Corporation which he describes as a non-Sheraton operation. This firm, according to Haddock, functions as a "catalyst" between the manufacturers of furnishings and the design staffs of hotel and motel chains. In talking of the relationship between a manufacturer and the Howard Johnson organization, Haddock said,

> The willingness of the manufacturer to develop furniture, draperies, and carpets along the lines that the designer wished to go turned out a very satisfactory result of which all could be proud. Here again, the design took the lead and eventually everything else became secondary.

Can the contract division staff member, surrounded by catalogs, make such a statement?

As a buyer, Haddock stresses the importance of price in volume buying. Speaking at a design seminar, he made this point in talking about a manufacturer whose designs were superlative.

> ... his price structure is geared to the small volume buyer of the home decorator market. He gets some business from us, but only a very small percentage of what he could get if his cost system were set up realistically. Without doubt, some goods are worth paying high prices for because of outstanding design. But this type

of buying never reaches a high volume. Design must be geared to price for the joint venture to succeed.

It is no secret that management will always try for a better price than the one quoted to the interior designer. And there seems to be no way of getting a manufacturer to set a price structure and stick to it. Discussing this subject, J. H. Leroy Chambers, president of the H. Chambers Company and a past president of the American Institute of Interior Designers, had this to say:

In my opinion, it is inequitable and not in the best interest of the manufacturer to quote varying discounts from list prices to recognized interior designers who represent today's largest contract market. My own company will not specify and purchase merchandise for a contract job unless we are convinced we are buying at the manufacturer's lowest F.O.B. factory price. We render every possible service to our clients and have clean cut efficient dealings with suppliers. Inasmuch as all invoices are paid within suppliers' terms, we feel a moral responsibility to our client for obtaining the manufacturer's lowest price. All established interior designers should be sold on the same discount basis. The manufacturer should do everything possible to support the interior design profession which, in turn, will make for an over-all healthy industry.

Take one of my contract clients for whom I'm working for a fee which is my profit for service that we render. Everything is open and above board. Our client knows where we are buying something, what the cost is, how it is made. This any client can find out and I don't care who the client may be. If he makes the effort, he can find out what the lowest price is. He wants the services of a top interior designer for all that it means and so in wanting it, he will pay a fee. But he should buy the merchandise at the right price.

The independent interior designer can usually buy fine furnishings cheaper than the hotel owner can. And he has sources and channels not open to the hotel owners. This has been overcome by the major hotel chains through the establishment of their own design and purchasing departments. To protect their retail outlets and the interior designers, many manufacturers refuse to sell directly to hotels. So the larger hotel companies set up independent buying offices under completely different names. These are run by people who know the market and can bargain for better prices on volume orders.

It is unlikely that any hotel chain dictates so strictly that its "independent" purchasing agents are forced to buy headboards from one certain source. But there are most certainly "preferred" manufacturers based on price and experience. Nevertheless, the interior designer working with a large chain in the development of a new hotel is usually given a certain amount of freedom of choice when it comes to sources because the owners realize the need of the hotel for individuality. If everything in the hotel comes from run-of-the-mill suppliers, the place will lack those special qualities that are so vital in attracting guests.

Take an item like the pictures on the walls of the guestrooms. Not too many years ago they were chosen by the housekeepers and it was almost a must that the picture be either a bowl of flowers, a harbor scene, or a seascape. Each of these pictures probably cost the hotel between $5 and $7. Today rather more thought goes into the choice of details like this. In the case of the Nile Hilton, for instance, we have seen what Welton Becket's design staff accomplished through the casting of bas relief reproductions from Babylonian and Egyptian museum pieces.

My own office often buys original paintings and has them silk screened. In this way, we are assured of offering the guest something special when he walks into his room. It provides a special tone and quality — such as might be found in a well decorated residence. Suitably framed, such a silk screen reproduction should cost the same as a good print of a Van Gogh or a Cezanne.

THE BATTLE OF THE BUDGET

In the public spaces of a hotel, it takes more than a reproduction to create an impact on the guest. In the Royal Orleans Hotel, there are many one-of-a-kind pieces, authentic antiques that the guests recognize immediately as being something very special. The acquisition of art objects obviously cannot be done routinely by a purchasing department. It must be left completely to the discretion of the interior designer. He will usually work hard to buy these special items at the very lowest price, but undoubtedly the purchasing agent for the owner winces when an antique mirror is purchased for $1,500. He is accustomed to paying $15 for mirrors, but that $1,500 one in the lobby is the thing that creates an area that is exciting and stimulating and that will make the guests remember the Royal Orleans. This particular project in New Orleans' French Quarter provides a good case history of an interior designer's role in the development of a new hotel. Though my office came into the job when the hotel was already under way, the story is fairly typical. Because the hotel had already been topped off, we inherited some other person's concepts. Some we had to live with because they were physically incorporated into the building.

Hotel Corporation of America executives changed designers because it was felt the original concept was too contemporary. They wanted something more suited to the Quarter with emphasis on the historical background and romance of the city. After preliminary conferences with the developers and management in New Orleans, we worked up a room count. This listed furniture requirements for each guestroom and the public spaces: so many beds, lamps, chests, and tables. Layouts for each area were submitted for approval.

The only major change came in the restaurants and bar to suit the traffic and service requirements of the management planners who wanted everything working out of one kitchen. This single kitchen is considered essential by many hotel men, but it does present problems in the traffic flow of different types of food. The Royal Orleans has a coffee shop, restaurant, rib room, and two bars.

When there are mistakes in the design of a hotel, they usually result from inadequate conferences between the architect, the designer and the operating staff of the hotel. In building a new hotel, the owner frequently waits too long in selecting a staff. As a result, no provision is made for adequate office space and storage.

William R. Ebersol
General Manager
Ambassador, Los Angeles

Once the layouts were approved, a final furniture count was taken together with statistics on draperies, wall coverings, carpeting, and the lighting fixtures. This work does not generally include dishes, silverware, and glassware, but we were at that early stage discussing color schemes with the independently hired graphics agency.

While the furniture count was going on, a model room was set up by our home office. This represented an investment of about $3,500 and was complete with walls and lighting fixtures. This is a common procedure today and serves the same purpose as the architect's model in giving both the designer and the client the opportunity of viewing the project in three dimensions. Client approval tends to be accelerated and, in addition, management can move the model room into the hotel where it can provide an excellent public relations tool.

There is one drawback to the practice of having specially designed furniture made up for a model room. The firms concerned go out on a limb in producing such samples. They do it, of course, in the hope of getting an order. However, the client's purchasing departments will often take the samples around to other manufacturers in an effort to get them at a lower price. This is only to be expected and it is doubtful if any ironbound protection for the craftsman is possible.

Final placement of orders for furniture is not always purely on the basis of price competition. It would be naive to ignore the effect on them of internal politics within the hotel firm and its purchasing department. There are simply too many ways of making a sale other than by pure price competition and the designer has no way of controlling the source, which is perhaps just as well. All the designer can do is show the sample of every item needed and let the purchasing department take it from there. Unfortunately, the quality is rarely as good as that of the sample. The most difficult task of the designer is to control quality and maintain some sort of minimum standard. His contract should give him the power to veto shoddy material. Without that power, he is in danger of having the job reflect on his professional reputation and ability. It is a touchy subject, but one the designers must face up to. Nor is this a fault confined to the large chains. Even with a small hotel job when there is no purchasing department to contend with, the owner will certainly have a friend in town who wants to sell something or a lodge brother who says his plant can copy any item and make it more cheaply.

There is no copyright in the world of design, but piracy must be combated and even a court case against it can sometimes be won.

Back to the battle of the budget. Once the model room has been approved and a count taken on layouts of public areas, a budget is submitted to management. The prices quoted are not arbitrary, but educated guesses based on experience. We know we can buy the type suggested at that price. Many times an item will be priced locally to get a guide line. For the Royal Orleans public spaces, a budget of $150,000 was submitted. Management cut this back to $140,000 and added $7,000 for contingencies. The budget for the guestrooms was submitted at $418,000. Furnishings for the suites were estimated at an additional $36,000. The figure of $1,200 per guestroom was reasonably firm but we knew that it would be easier to trim the budget here than in any other part of the hotel. When saving is possible on hardware for case goods, or on fabrics, or on any other quantity item, then a reduction of $50 or more per room is not inconceivable. In a hotel of several hundred rooms, such a saving multiplies into classical figures.

It is probably safe to say that most designers move to the high side of a budget to provide a hedge when the negotiating gets tough. Management invariably says everything is too expensive no matter what prices are proposed.

With the budget finally approved and feelings soothed, then is the time to get down to the specifics of choosing furniture and start requisitioning. Actual sources and unit costs are added to the budget control sheet. This then goes to the management's purchasing agent in requisition form. He can either approve it or start shopping himself. About ten per cent of the furnishings for the Royal Orleans were left open as to source and price because our office knew these items would be shopped by the purchasing department in Boston. We knew from experience that certain items would come from management's special sources. But even when suggested sources are approved, management will usually make an attempt to secure a better price than the one quoted to the designer. This is all a part of proper business management; the man who does not touch all the bases will find himself off the team.

THE ELUSIVE OPENING

Then comes the logistics of installation and the staggering of delivery dates to fit exactly into the schedules set up by the architect and contractor.

In general, furnishings are shipped directly to the guestrooms. If the job is running behind schedule, the convention hall or meeting rooms can be used for storage to save warehousing costs. Carpeting and draperies are handled by installation firms hired by the fabricators. It is their responsibility to prevent shortages and to check for damage. Experienced installation crews can save the designer countless headaches as opening day nears. In the case of the Royal Orleans, the draperies were fabricated in Boston, trucked to the hotel, and modified on the site as required. The same system is used for the banquettes in the dining rooms. The fabricator sends his own men to the job site to make measurements which are then checked against the architect's working drawings.

Before the age of the jet airliner, proximity to the job was considered a must for the architect, designer, and suppliers. Today one is as close to any hotel as the nearest airport. Even when the project site is far from his home office, the interior designer can stay as close to it as if it were an hour's drive away. This is true also of hotel work overseas through the use of a tape recorder and the Polaroid camera. In my own assignments in North Africa, Bermuda, and England, the team captain for a hotel project keeps me posted daily with snapshots. Tapes are an invaluable tool for keeping in touch with daily problems.

THE IMPORTANCE OF LIGHTING

Lighting plays a major role in hotel design today, especially in public spaces. Flexibility of space is recognized as being vital and lighting is important in achieving multiplicity of use in public rooms. An independent lighting consultant is indispensable for hotel work. It is usually a mistake to rely on a consultant employed by fixture manufacturers because he is most likely to be limited in his freedom of selection. He would be forced to sell his own fixtures and I do not know of any one manufacturer who could supply a complete specification from his catalog. Some are better on decorative fixtures. Others have the edge in optics. Consultants employed by the major bulb manufacturers are interested in the output and quantity of light; often in a hotel, what is wanted is smaller quantities of quality light.

Lighting was one of our first concerns in the Royal Orleans and we brought in a consultant immediately to determine the limitations and the opportunities of the electrical system and layout. One very expensive chandelier had already been ordered, but no commitments for finish materials had been made.

The independently hired lighting consultant may be an absolute genius, but he still must start with something to light. He must be told what effects are desired and with what textures he will be working. The designer must explain what moods are to be achieved, but never should he attempt to dictate how this is to be done. He should point out the features of the hotel that are to be accented by lighting, but not attempt to set the method.

A lighting consultant will first show preliminary sketches of what he intends to do. This is necessary to make sure he is not accentuating something the designer would rather keep in the shadows. Guestroom lighting is a more simple task and one that the interior designer usually works out for himself. But a consultant is able to provide valuable advice for lighting such areas as corridors where lighting can play an architectural role.

The designer must depend on sketches to translate his concepts for the lighting expert: words too often prove nebulous. A similar inability to communicate bedevils many designers' relationships with architects and engineers and a similar solution is possible. With sketches, the designer can show the lighting consultant what atmospheres and moods are needed. In the case of restaurants and bars, several sketches may be necessary to show how the room will change its mood from breakfast to late evening.

The writer has a strong dislike of the fluorescent tube and could live without this light source except for such special cases as large office areas, or background or in limited spaces where the incandescent lamp could not do the job. Control of fluorescent light is extremely limited, no matter what type it may be: it lacks warmth, softness, and the flattering effect of the incandescent light. It seems highly probable that if the incandescent lamp had come along after, instead of before the fluorescent tube, people would hail it as the greatest thing that ever happened in the lighting industry.

Bill Richardson of Jaros, Baum and Bolls in New York, has the following do's and don'ts in the matter of hotel lighting:

1. In general, do not use fluorescent light in public areas. The only exceptions are sample rooms and the front desk. Fluorescence can be used

occasionally for decorative emphasis, such as was used for back-lighting screens at the Carlton Tower in London.

2. Where a linear source of light is necessary, use cold cathode. The colors are more satisfactory and the dimming characteristics are better.

3. Do not use yellow or amber colored bulbs or filters for lighting people, food, or liquor. These colors can be used sparingly for decorative accents and background mood lighting.

4. Use pink for lighting people and creating a warm and inviting atmosphere, but be careful not to use too intense a pink that will distort rather than compliment. Use lavender or pale pink filters in rooms where food is served. Lavender in particular enhances all foods as well as complexions.

5. Use all other colors sparingly and generally to create moods, for backgrounds to orchestras, to accent planting, and for lighting shows.

6. Fluorescent light can be used in bathrooms because of its efficiency, but use properly colored tubes such as soft white and natural white.

7. Do not use fluorescent light in corridors. Incandescent in general and wall brackets in particular create a warmer and more home-like atmosphere.

8. Use dimmers in all public rooms, particularly those in which more than one type of function will take place. Where the budget is a problem, dimmers can be eliminated from the bar provided no food is served and in the coffee shop provided it is not used for any other type of function. Generally speaking, dimmers are not necessary for lobbies.

Looking into the future of hotel design, Richardson sees electro-luminescence playing an important role as a new source of light. He feels designers will have to re-orient their approach in order to use this light source properly. Experimentation today indicates problems with color and Richardson feels there will be only limited use made of electronic panels.

Gazing into the blue sky depths, the lighting expert predicts the use of dimmers controlled by sound waves. The hotel guest will be able to regulate all lighting in the room without moving from his chair.

Otherwise, the future lies in the imagination of all designers concerned with architecture, decor, and lighting.

ANSWERS TO HARD QUESTIONS

I think that designers in general overlook some of the practical aspects of their task. We have found that particularly true of carpeting that gets dirty very quickly and of dark carpeting that gets spotty and stained. This weakness of being impractical leads to maintenance costs and efforts that are tremendous.

A. M. Sonnabend, President
Hotel Corporation of America

In the countless interviews conducted during the preparation of this book, the most provocative answers came in dealing with mistakes that "the other fellow" most often makes. The late Barney Allis, owner of the Muehlebach in Kansas City, minced no words.

There are no perfectly designed hotels in the world, or even any that are near perfect. And that goes for the new ones.

Allis complained that architects and designers do not seem to understand hotel problems from the ground up.

If you were going to design a city, where would you start? You'd start with traffic. And the same thing holds true for a hotel.

He also felt that the trouble with most hotels is their lack of variety in what they have to offer. He was very proud of his Muehlebach because the rooms possess a high degree of convertibility.

> Having a thousand rooms doesn't necessarily mean anything because I can have only 700 and have more merchandise that will sell. We don't decorate them all pink or blue, either. If you were to open a men's clothing shop, you wouldn't fill up all the racks with black suits. It is the convertible room that makes for an efficient hotel operation. That way we have very few that are strictly sleepers.

Obviously, there are sound business arguments on the side of uniformity with a high minimum standard, but Mr. Allis made a good point in opposition.

Another management viewpoint, from William Ebersol of the Ambassador in Los Angeles, blames mistakes on inadequate conferences between architect-designer and the operating staff of the hotel. In Ebersol's view:

> In building a new hotel, the owner frequently waits too long in selecting a staff. As a result, no provision is made for adequate office, staff and storage space. Also, the architect and/or designer frequently represents that he is experienced in hotel work, when in fact the finished job would have been more satisfactory had he brought in associates and consultants actively engaged in various hotel services and acquainted with the area in which the hotel is being built.

The question of adequate non-rentable space came up in an interview with the management team at the Plaza Hotel in New York. Neal Lang, who was manager during the restoration program in the early 1960s, made the point that in older hotels such as the Plaza, there are problems with lack of elevators, lack of storage space for supplies and lack of locker rooms and facilities for the staff. "These are the things that are so important when you go out to hire people," Lang said. Arthur Dooley, who was then Lang's assistant, spelled out the problem created by the shrinking budget.

> Designers can accomplish a great deal in the original concept, he said, but in the end, the operator winds up with problems because after the ideas get on paper and are designed to work properly, it turns out the whole thing is over the budget and it then becomes a job to squeeze all the necessary items into X number of dollars. That is when the so-called fat gets squeezed out of the program. You cut back on the non-revenue producing areas, the very locker rooms you need to keep employees satisfied, the kitchen and the storage space, and finally you find yourself making the guest-rooms a little smaller.

Lang added that it was like the man who needs a size ten shoe, but is told to buy an eight. He cannot walk properly. He develops sore feet and is forced to see a chiropodist to have the painful corns removed. And eventually he has to go back and buy the size tens.

Much has been written about the availability of expert advice for the hotel industry, but this is no insurance against making serious mistakes in building a new hotel. Lang recalled that he was running the Cadillac Hotel in Detroit when the Sheraton chain was preparing to build its first new hotel in downtown Philadelphia. Every manager of a Sheraton hotel received a letter that started off with words to this effect: "If you had the privilege of getting everything you wanted in a new hotel, what are the things you would ask for first?"

Lang's answer to the home office dealt primarily with adequate elevator service, storage space and convenient kitchens. He recalled that

> Despite the advice from all those managers, Sheraton went ahead
> and built the banquet hall and grand ballroom primarily depend-
> ent on escalator service from the street. Somebody at Sheraton
> headquarters had decided that everybody coming to a banquet
> would be coming in off the street, never giving it a thought that
> some of the people in those 400 guestrooms would be heading for
> the same place. So within a year, they were tearing out guestrooms
> to install extra elevator facilities. It's pretty serious when a fun-
> damental mistake is made by a corporation with the resources
> and research staff that Sheraton has.

RUFUS NIMS' REMARKS

Particularly provocative were the comments of Miami architect Rufus Nims whose research for Howard Johnson was discussed in the earlier chapter on motor hotels. Nims complained that most designers seem con-cerned only with embellishing space, putting objects and finishes in an acceptable arrangement.

Perhaps he was speaking tongue in cheek when he said ninety-nine per cent of the assignments designers receive are in relatively bad build-ings.

> The better architects prefer to do their own interiors. Can you
> imagine turning the average decorator loose on a building by
> Frank Lloyd Wright, Mies van der Rohe or Corbusier? It would
> not work because that decorator is not trained to think in terms
> of spaces and their basic relationships.

It is unfortunate that what Nims says is true in so many cases. Despite the growing stature of the interior design field, there still are many in the profession who do not have the training and who are simply choosers of furnishings. From the designer's point of view, the worst moments come when the client develops a case of nerves half way through the job. Accord-ing to Sam Revness,

> The owner's most serious mistake in dealing with a designer is not
> letting him go ahead with the hotel as it was planned; in not
> demonstrating confidence in his own choice of the designer. When
> a client starts to dictate the policy of design, then he is confessing
> he picked the wrong person for the job.

Revness warns that on such a project, the result is a compromise between the designer's talents and the non-educated guesses of the owner. Obviously it is the owner who must decide how much money is to be spent, he said,

> but the owner certainly should not start picking out colors and fabrics. When he starts doing that, he has the wrong designer and the designer has the wrong client.

I have already confessed my grand failure with the pseudo Spanish hotel in Miami Beach. It was the result of my following the owner down a primrose path that was thick with thorns. The same thing might have happened also in the case of the Motel de Ville in New Orleans, but here I felt sure of myself and I pulled up sharply on the reins. The wife of one of the owners wanted to help with the interiors. Her taste was based solely on experiences with her own home and I had seen her home so I knew my opponent. It was filled with reproductions of French Provincial and the various and sundry Louies so, naturally, she felt I was making the hotel too modern and that the colors would be too dramatic. Her interference was concentrated mainly in the guestrooms because she could relate her experience with this amount of space; the size of the public areas made them too much for her to grasp.

The problem was solved simply by asking her and her husband to sit down with me and discuss the situation openly. I told them I had been hired because they had seen examples of my work and had liked what they saw. I explained that while a hotel had to have certain home-like qualities, these had no relationship with the decorating scheme in the client's home. I stressed the point that when you make a mistake in the interior design of a hotel guestroom, it is deadly serious because the error is multiplied by the number of key boxes at the front desk.

It is useless for the designer to argue with the client about things like colors or fabrics in the middle of a job. It would be as senseless as arguing with a woman about her costume when she is half dressed. You can't tell then how she is going to look when she walks out the door with the accouterment of gloves, accessories, and the final combing of the hair. Unfortunately, the old adage applies here: never show a fool something that is half finished.

Calling a client a fool is harsh language, but you can't get away from the fact it is impossible for the person who is unfamiliar with interior design to appreciate how a room will look when it is completed. Even with renderings which pretty much show how a room will look when the mirrors and draperies are installed, it is difficult for a client to visualize the results and to maintain a hands-off attitude when he is disturbed by the job at a midway point.

It is also understandable that the investor might get cold feet as the hotel nears completion. He might start to have misgivings about the success of the hotel. He worries that people will not like it. He wonders if it might not be safer to hold back on some of his capital. This is when the interior designer must be prepared to show the client that the only prudent thing to do is complete the hotel as it was originally planned. The cake without icing is the last one sold in the bakery.

Submitting renderings of hotel rooms, the designer should beware of making them so glamorous that the client is destined for disappointment when the work is completed. There are two different types of renderings. One is the prospectus which is always very dramatic. It is rarely like the finished room will be, but it does serve as a selling tool. However, the second type, a factual rendering without pretense, causes considerably less trouble in the long run.

Some brief mention has been made of graphics for a hotel. The responsibility for this phase of design usually rests with an advertising agency hired by the client, but the interior designer should take part in the creation of a motif that will dominate in areas of promotion and imagery. Graphics help to establish the personality of a hotel and must be carried out carefully from the design of the menu to that of the matchbook cover that guests will carry to all parts of the world.

Howard Heinsius, vice president of Needham and Grohmann, told a management workshop at Cornell University that this principle of coordination is fundamental to all good advertising. Moreover, he said,

> It is good taste as well as good business. You wouldn't decorate your guestrooms or your dining room in six or eight colors. Why do it with advertising and promotional materials?

The advertising executive told the hotel men that coordination in motif, design, and color makes advertising instantly recognizable and multiplies its impact on the reader and potential guest.

Erwin Harris, who heads one of the largest advertising agencies in Florida, has become a specialist in creating graphics for resort hotels. He was hired at the same time as the architects in the planning of the Fontainebleau, the Eden Roc, and the Americana Hotels in Miami Beach. Harris starts with the name, searching for something that will be distinctive. Then comes the logotype which must be memorable. In his view:

> The logotype must reveal the style of the hotel, it must establish a feeling and a personality. More important, when it runs in the newspapers and magazines, it must be highly legible and immediately identifiable.

Harris strives for the remembrance factor in his design of graphics and emphasizes:

> It doesn't always have to be a romantic remembrance as you need for a resort hotel, but it must be distinctive.

Years ago, the commercial hotel had only to open its doors and wait for the people to start arriving. Management today must go out in search of luncheon business, banquets, and conventions. It is here that graphics plays an important part.

Harris believes the commercial hotel must achieve high style in its graphics without getting into high fashion. There is a big difference. The latter may be fine in a resort hotel, but there must be no hint of femininity for the commercial house. Promotional material for the downtown hotel should be masculine, very forthright and direct. This type of approach should also be taken by the resort hotel in its special material designed for convention business needed in the off-season. Harris urges that such material be so detailed that it can serve as a direct selling tool. It must tell the convention selection committee everything about the hotel; exactly how many persons a meeting room or banquet hall will accommodate. These convention pieces must be engineering studies when it comes to floor plans and dimensions. Yet the material must also show how attractive the hotel is so that wives of delegates will be anxious to make the trip. Says Harris:

> A hotel that offers only rooms today cannot stand up to competition. There are X number of persons who will go on vacation or take business trips. The agency responsible for graphics and advertising must try to get for its clients more than their normal share of that business.

While Harris personally believes in choosing a hotel name suited to the modern idiom, he has been involved with the development of resort hotels that are champions of pretentiousness. In the case of the Fontainebleau, the brochures cost fifty cents each and were tricked out with a set of gates on the cover. The advertising man is not without a defense.

> A hotel like the Fontainebleau with its marble, statuary and elaborate candelabra called for graphics to match. I would have done the owner a disservice had I come up with clean and modern graphics.

trinidad hilton

Virgin isle Hilton

Mayaguez Hilton

DIPLOMAT

Beverly Rodeo Hotel

aruba caribbean

A study of the trade marks on the previous two pages will point up the way various designers have solved the problem of identity. A more complete graphics program is shown starting on page 190.

In the case of a major hotel, graphics involves a comprehensive program of planning and execution. But even with a 50-room motel, the owner should buy top quality art work for his logotype. Nor does he have to go to a flossy agency. A competent commercial artist or a designer can produce an attractive logotype for advertising, stationery, and the sign out front. The smallest hotel needs that as a minimum to establish a personality for itself.

John Carden Campbell, partner in the architectural firm of Campbell and Wong, warns that turning a motel or hotel into a high billboard with blinking neon and flashing arrows will certainly attract the eye of the motorist, but it won't necessarily attract a customer. "Will he feel an enjoyable stay is possible in a motel that screams its presence with gaudy signs and colors?" Campbell asks. Motel developers crowding into key intersections of the new federal highway program should ask themselves the same question.

These are fiercely competitive times for hotel and motel men. The customers may pass by the pretentious place, but they will never ignore the one that is well designed and presents a pleasing image. The combination of good architect, good interior designer, and good graphics director will always produce an exceptional product. These are the persons who not only know what must be put into a hotel but more important, they know what needs to be left out.

The bromide of "selling the sizzle, not the steak" belongs to a bygone day. Success now belongs to the man who sells the prime steak properly prepared and graciously served.

The Rehabilitation Work Schedule chart shown on the next two pages was prepared from one that the Duo-Bid Corporation had made up.

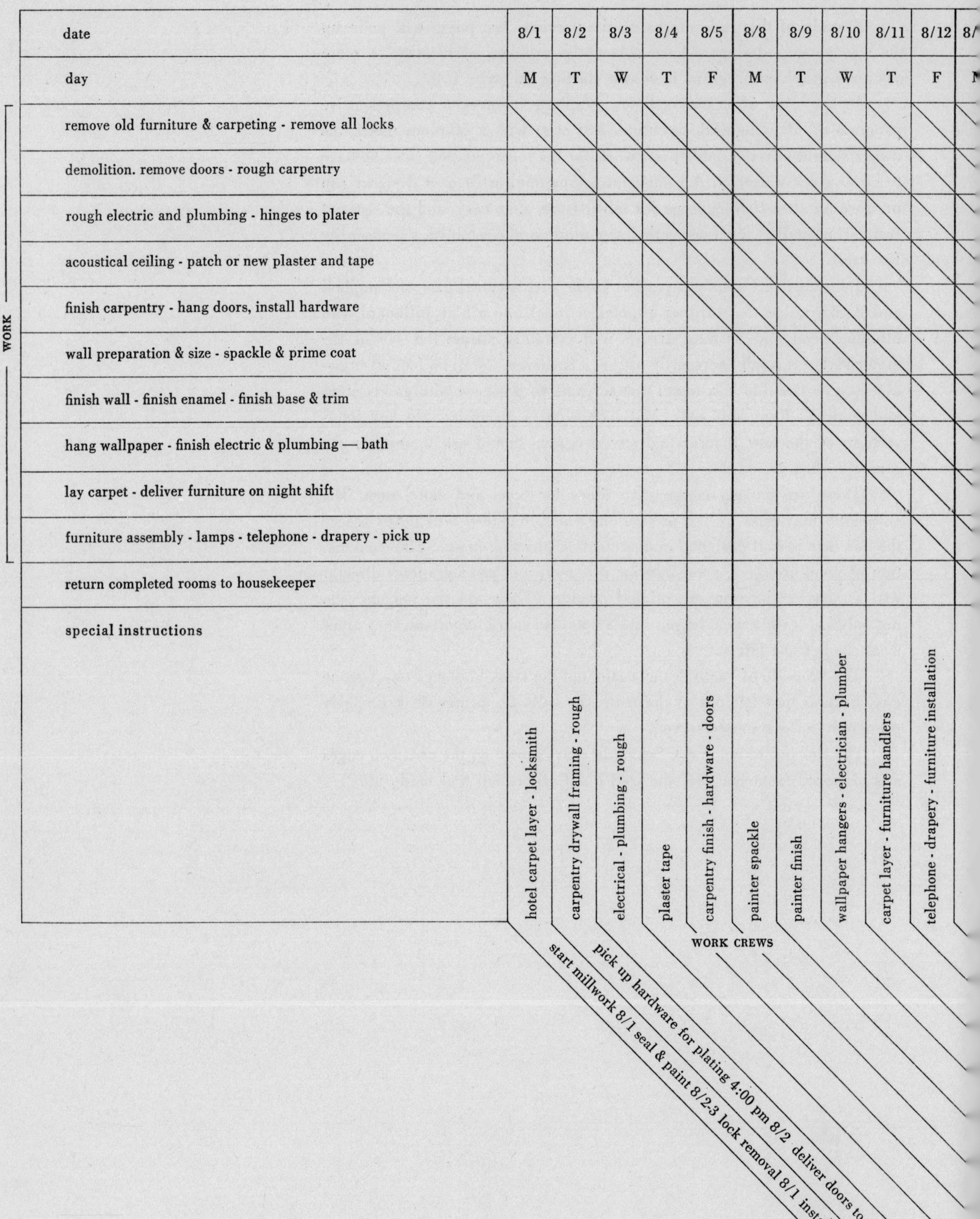

date	8/1	8/2	8/3	8/4	8/5	8/8	8/9	8/10	8/11	8/12	8/
day	M	T	W	T	F	M	T	W	T	F	M
remove old furniture & carpeting - remove all locks											
demolition. remove doors - rough carpentry											
rough electric and plumbing - hinges to plater											
acoustical ceiling - patch or new plaster and tape											
finish carpentry - hang doors, install hardware											
wall preparation & size - spackle & prime coat											
finish wall - finish enamel - finish base & trim											
hang wallpaper - finish electric & plumbing — bath											
lay carpet - deliver furniture on night shift											
furniture assembly - lamps - telephone - drapery - pick up											
return completed rooms to housekeeper											
special instructions											

WORK

WORK CREWS

- hotel carpet layer - locksmith
- carpentry drywall framing - rough
- electrical - plumbing - rough
- plaster tape
- carpentry finish - hardware - doors
- painter spackle
- painter finish
- wallpaper hangers - electrician - plumber
- carpet layer - furniture handlers
- telephone - drapery - furniture installation

pick up hardware for plating 4:00 pm 8/2 deliver doors to mill 8/2

start millwork 8/1 seal & paint 8/2-3 lock removal 8/1 install 8/5

/16	8/17	8/18	8/19	8/22	8/23	8/24	8/25	8/26	8/29	9/1	9/2	9/3	9/4
T	W	T	F	M	T	W	T	F	M	T	W	T	F

ROOMS

Room labels (diagonal):
rm 909 · 10 · 12 · 14 · 16 · 17 · 18 · 19 · 20
rm (922-24-26) 28 · 30 · 31 · 32 · 33 · 34 · 35
rm 936 · 38 · 40 · 42 · 44 · 46 · 48 · 41 · 43 · 45
rm 950 · 52 · 47 · 49   rm 809 · 10 · 12 · 14 · 16 · 17
rm 818 · 19 (820-22-24-26) 28 · 30 · 31 · 32
rm 833 · 34 · 36 · 36 · 38 · 40 · 42 · 48 · 41 · 43
rm 850 · 52 · 54 · 45 · 47 · 56 · 49 · 58   709 · 710
rm 712 · 14 · 16 · 17 · 18 · 19 · 20 · 22 · 24 · 26
rm 728 · 30 · 31 · 32 · 33 · 34 · 35 · 36 · 38 · 40
rm 742 · (44-46) · 41 · 43 · 45 · 47 · 56 · 49 · 58
rm 609 · 10 · 12 · 14 · 16 · 17 · 18 · 19 · 20 · 22
rm 624 · 26 · 28 · 30 · 31 · 32 · 33 · 34 · 35 · 36
rm 638 · 40 · 42 · 48 · 41 · 50 · 52 · 43 · 45 · 54
rm series 11   series 37   special treatment

REHABILITATION WORK SCHEDULE

It is possible to rehabilitate over a hundred rooms in a period of five weeks or 25 working days by setting up a schedule of this kind. Each series of rooms is out of service for only two weeks. Each crew of workmen moves along from one set of rooms through to the last in orderly fashion. In addition, it will be noted that those rooms requiring special treatment are saved until last in case any problems arise.

219

VIII – PROSPECTS

Illustrations

The text for this Chapter will be found on pages 237 to 241

PROSPECTS

Hotel America, Boston, Massachusetts. Scheduled for opening in early 1965, this will be Boston's first new hotel in 30 years and certainly its largest, with 1,000 rooms on 27 floors plus extensive convention and meeting facilities, four specialty dining rooms, and a huge garage. Designed as three hotels in one, the America will combine the facilities of a luxurious residential tower, a convention meeting hotel, and a drive-in resort motel as part of the high complex planned by the Prudential Insurance Company in Boston's Back Bay area. Individual staffs and separate entrances will serve each of the divisions of the new hotel. One important aspect of the America is that it will allow Boston to compete for large convention groups that previously could not be accommodated because of the city's lack of adequate group meeting and dining facilities.

Architecture: Charles Luckman Associates
Consultants to Architect: Henry End Associates
Interiors: Roland Jutras

The extensive program of new hotels by Loews includes this 370-room hotel at Eighth Avenue and 48th Street in New York City. It is designed to serve the average motorist rather than the expense-account executive.

Architecture and interiors: Lapidus Liebman Associates

222

Above. Probable flagship for the numerous hotels that are being built in the nation's capital will be the gigantic Washington Hilton. Architecture: William B. Tabler

Penn Center Inn represents a trend in high-rise motels in congested down-town areas, based on the idea of providing convenience at an in-city location, room for a parking garage on the second and third levels, with slightly inclined ramps allowing 250 motorists to self-park. They will register at the entrance, remaining in their cars if they wish, and after parking can handle their own bags on a push cart, taking a self-service elevator to their room. It is also the product of a cooperative method of design in which owner, manager, building architect, and interior designer worked as a team from the beginning of the project.

Architecture: Charles Luckman Associates
Interiors: Henry End Associates

223

As part of an extensive development program for tourism, four hotels are being built in Tunisia. Illustration of one of them on the island of Djerba indicates the romantic architectural approach utilizing traditional furnishings with modern techniques. Lobby illustrates contemporary interior architecture combined with the use of furnishings that embrace North African flavor.

Architecture: Mr. Levadowsky, Mr. Demenais,
Mr. Cacoub, and
Mr. Boulakbeche
Interiors: Henry End Associates
Associates: Vernes and
Pierre Deshay

The New York Hilton at Rockefeller Center has over 2,000 guest rooms. The building is 45 floors above grade and towers 487 feet above street level. The guest tower is served by high-speed, automatic passenger elevators in three banks and the suites and room service generally are handled by five automatic, high speed elevators. Escalators connect the concourse level, lobby floor, mezzanine, and second floor. Although the entire architectural concept was William B. Tabler's, three interior designers have been employed — William Pahlmann for dining areas, Joe Mielziner for the ballroom, and Joseph Huston for the guest rooms.

San Francisco Hilton. Designed by William B. Tabler, this hotel is scheduled for opening in 1963.

S · HARLE · B · LIEBMAN
INTERIOR DESIGNERS

226

Prudential Center. Artist's rendering of the ball-room which will seat more than 1,000. Specially designed ceiling integrates lighting, acoustics, and air conditioning.

Top, facing page. The brand-new Americana in San Juan is a resort hotel specifically geared to group and convention facilities. Its banquet and meeting rooms can accommodate 2,500 guests and private conference and dining rooms are also provided.
Architecture and Interiors: Morris Lapidus, Harle & Liebman

Bottom, facing page. Adjoining Los Angeles International Airport, these residential styled buildings will combine complete resort facilities with comfortable stopover guest rooms for those traveling by air or automobile.
Architecture: Welton Becket and Associates.

Hotel Lucayan, Freeport, Grand Bahamas. Above. As part of an extensive program of developing the Grand Bahamas, the luxury Hotel Lucayan is being built to lure tourists from other Caribbean vacation spots. Two of the main attractions will be gambling and duty-free shopping. Public spaces and guest rooms have been designed to combine native materials and contemporary furnishings.
Architecture. Herb Matthes.
Interiors: Henry End Associates.

Right. Howard Johnson's downtown Washington Motor Lodge is a far cry from their typical, gabled, red-tiled roof. Featured will be a 900 square foot roof top swimming pool, roof garden, and cocktail lounge with a view of the Capitol.
Architecture: Chatelain, Gauges, and Nolan.

The Southern Cross at Melbourne, Australia exemplifies the massive American-styled hotel structure, combining guest rooms, specialty dining, and convention facilities.
Architecture: Welton Becket and Associates.

As part of the Southwest Urban Renewal Program in Washington, D.C., the Skyline Motor Inn, designed by Lapidus, Liebman Associates is being built. The result of a contest won by the architect on the basis of best development plan submitted, it is designed specifically for the motoring public. It will have two basic entrances: one of more conventional type for use of motorists; the other, the main entrance, with no typical front door but separated from the outdoors by an air curtain of hot or cold air, depending on outdoor temperature.

Hotel America, Houston, Texas. This 300-room hotel is part of Cullen Center, a complex of office buildings, apartments, and shopping center. The interior designer was given the opportunity to build prototype guest rooms and worked with the architects right through the early concept, a method strongly to be recommended for it creates an atmosphere of harmonious cooperation.

Architecture: Welton Becket and Associates.

Interiors: Henry End Associates.

ROOMS OF TOMORROW, 1959 TO 1963

The first "Room of Tomorrow" was shown at the International Hotel Exposition in 1959 held at the New York Coliseum. The original idea was that a number of manufacturers would showcase new products within an integrated designed hotel room, demonstrating new concepts for the hotel guest room. Since that time the idea has lost purpose and it is now no more than a sample bureau of products unrelated to the possibilities of using the prototype itself. The last "Room of Tomorrow", the 1963 one, would cost an operator, were he to utilize the ideas and furnishings, over $10,000 per room.

1959

Designer: Henry End Associates

Entry, bath, living-sleeping area, and terrace comprise this first "Room of Tomorrow." Furniture is concentrated at perimeters to leave floor space free; box spring beds look like sofas, mirrors are used to magnify space, and luminescent walls rather than space-cluttering lamps have all been used to get maximum duality of use as both sleeping and living area. The bathroom is separated into three compartments by sliding doors of amethyst glass and plastic covered with Persian Fretwork.

1960

Designer: Tom Lee, Ltd.

Space-saving plan, versatile furniture, and easily-maintained materials are the features of the 1960 "Room of Tomorrow."

Above right. Storage units (available in ready-made components) covered with Parkwood's Rosewood laminate form a convex curve across the living-sleeping room. The units contain closet, dressing table, chest, television set, desk, and serving pantry. The cocktail table divides into two semi-circular night tables.

Right. From the terrace the sofa-beds can be seen in their daytime position. At night they are swivelled 90° into the room whereupon the high padded arms become headboards. In the five-sided cabinet between the two are remote controls for television, rdaio, and built-in telephone with night light and answer button.

1961

Designer: Marion Hoyer, A.I.D.

Ingenious use of new products and materials in this "Room of Tomorrow" went far to provide guests with space for dining, working, and relaxing as well as for sleeping.

Above. Through the sliding glass doors of the terrace the whole room is visible. Mainly by use of color and materials, the designer has created separate areas for various activities in what is little larger than a conventional guestroom space. To the rear right a dining area is formed by a floor curve of Amtico's vinyl "Textura;" the kitchen behind it is enclosed by folding doors of reinforced transluscent plastic.

Left. Random buckled belts of vinyl fabric form a room divider between large sofa-bed and dresser, all part of a unit containing storage space. The print is backed up by a mirror over the dresser. Here the bed is pulled out; by day it rolls back into a recess in the bureau with a sofa back as part of the divider unit. The "headboard" is a decorative wall plaque and beside it are a control center for television, air conditioner, and dimmers, plus a Bell Speakerphone with light and amplifier.

1962

Designer: Emily Malino, A.I.D.

The 1962 "Room of Tomorrow" is a DeLuxe Double unit with living room and bedrooms separated by a split floor level as well as by decorative treatment. The Double can sleep two adults (in the bedroom) and two children(on the sofa hide-a-bed in the living room).

Above. In the living room as seen from the bedroom step-down, the facing sofa sleeps two. The color scheme is restful but by no means dull — olive, beige, rose, and melon spiced with Tangerine and green. Clever lighting and furniture arrangement gives spaciousness in an actually quite compact area.

Right. The bedroom area as seen from the living room. A subtle change in color which does not disturb the over-all scheme helps differentiate the two areas. The beds are motor-adjustable to any angle for reading, television-watching, or breakfast in bed.

234

1963

Designer: Roy Beal, F.A.I.D.

The 1963 "Room of Tomorrow" consisted of two separate projects: a luxury suite called "Room at the Top" and the "Short-Stop Room" for the overnight or between-planes guest. On this page are pictures from the former which was composed of a bathroom, and a bedroom and living room separated by a foyer and the interjecting bar of a T-shaped loggia.

Above. The foyer as seen from the loggia entrance with living room to the left and bedroom to the right. The tapestry, by Gilles A. Briaux, hangs behind the bar with a wall phone, coffee-maker, and enclosed refrigerator unit. Vinyl gives a mat-like floor covering.

Left. In the bedroom the furniture has a period look absent from the other areas of the suite. King-size bed, formal draperies, and perforated polished brass light cones add a touch of drama to the room.

The "Short-Stop Room," 10 feet x 12 feet in size, is furnished compactly and functionally. Materials, though practical, are gay and luxurious; the sofa-bed has a laminated arm extension for writing or dining; and the shell arm chair serves as a desk, dining, or extra chair.

235

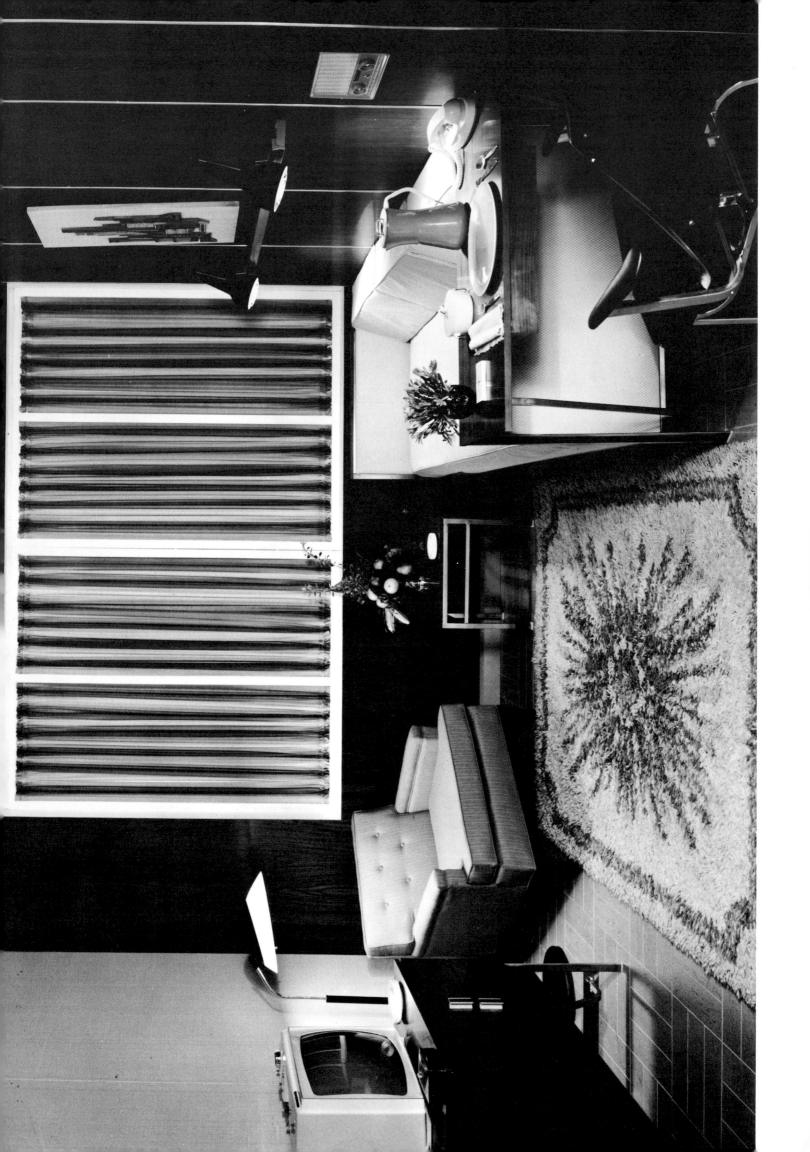

VIII—PROSPECTS

"What's past is prologue," said the Duke of Milan in Shakespeare's *Tempest* in an utterance particularly appropriate to our theme. Consider the storm of controversy that breaks out with every spurt of new construction in the hotel industry. It is highly probable that the man who built the second stagecoach inn near London was accused of trying to wreck the economy.

Fifteen years after the "No Vacancy" prosperity of the World War II years, the American hotel industry shuddered at forecasts of ruinous competition from new metropolitan hotels and motels. The trade press and the accountants charged with taking regular pulse checks hammered home their warnings like a broken record. In January, 1962, the *Hotel World-Review* ran a headline: "Hotel Occupancies Skid, Yet They Keep Building More."

For five years, hotels and motor hotels had been coming out of the ground at the rate of about half a billion dollars worth a year. This was mild compared to the 1920s when the rate was three times as great, but each year the cry grew louder that new hotels were simply accelerating the drop in occupancy rates and that a breathing spell was needed to take up the slack. The general feeling seemed akin to that of the characters in Rodgers' and Hammerstein's musical *Oklahoma!* about Kansas City — that they had "gone about as far as they could go." But the hotel business has always been a dynamic one and so it will remain; the problems of obsolete hotels will not be solved by halting the construction of new ones.

Pointing to the great washout of hotel investments during the depression of the 1930s will not obviate the fact that in the 1960s most metropolitan areas have a shortage of modern guestrooms and convention facilities, despite the billions that have been spent on new hotels since World War II. Statistics on overall occupancy rates for the industry are useful research tools, but one must look behind the ledger sheet to find out which hotels are doing better than the average, and why.

Years ago, hotel managers considered themselves lucky if they broke even on food and beverage operations. Today, with automation in the kitchen and an aggressive convention sales force on the road year-round, a new hotel's banquet rooms and specialty restaurants are contributing heavily to net income. In older hotels, the guest can spend ten minutes looking for a place to get a drink. In the new hotels, a strict teetotaler will find himself draped over a leather upholstered bar if he comes through the front door with any degree of momentum.

One of the major problems today, I call "keeping up with the Joneses," and with new model motor hotels coming out annually like automobiles, it is difficult and most expensive for the old property to keep up with the new facilities and services.

Richard B. Ziegler
Pick Hotels Corporation

Owners of old hotels must realize that their problem is not only with the new competition, but with the tens of thousands of dollars they spend every year dusting rubber plants and renaissance moldings in lobbies and gloomy writing rooms that resemble something out of the Charles Addams cartoons. While all that dusting is going on in old hotels, new ones are using the lobby as a shuttle station to move guests by automatic elevators and escalators to a variety of atmospheres designed to put them in a happy (and spending) frame of mind.

Instead of worrying about competition for obsolete rooms, development commissions in metropolitan areas must recognize that hotels with modern facilities are essential to attract conventions; and it is among convention delegates that cities will find the men who control industrial expansion in America. It would be difficult to deny that the migration of industry to South Florida was related to the growth of convention business in Miami Beach. As we have seen, in Puerto Rico the government financed the Caribe Hilton to make a positive impression on the American business leader on vacation. This kind of thing is happening in all parts of the world because a new hotel is a symbol of progress. Not only that, it is an economic necessity. And it is true for New York City as it is for Karachi or Addis Ababa.

Perhaps the statistics compiled by the American Hotel Association would prove that in 1962 Manhattan did not need any more hotel rooms. But those same figures take no account of the number of antiquated guestrooms so shabby that they stay empty more than half the time and pull the national occupancy down to the level the industry finds so disturbing.

New York has always been one of the major convention cities in the nation, but it never got its rightful share of the big national meetings because it lacked hotels with the enormous meeting rooms necessary for such functions. The Tisch brothers' Americana and the Uris-Hilton hotel were both designed to fill that need. In his autobiography, written in the mid 1950s, Conrad Hilton recalled a speech he had made to Michigan State students in which he predicted hotels comparable to the Waldorf and the old Stevens in Chicago would never again be built in any country. He forecast that new hotels would be smaller in size, a thousand rooms or less,

When we built the International Hotel at Idlewild Airport, we decided 320 rooms was just about right for that area. But before we knew it, there were three motels with a total of 276 rooms all around us. If this keeps up, people will start cutting pricing and everyone will suffer.

William B. Rasor
Executive Vice President
Knott Hotels

of a design that will help bridge the gap between luxurious personal service and the necessity of keeping the price within reasonable limits.

But only a few years later, Hilton joined in the construction of a 45-story tower of glass and steel containing 2,165 rooms. "A living showcase for the best in American design and crafts," he called the New York Hilton when the two-year project got underway in 1961.

An interesting point in the development of the New York Hilton was the use of different designers for various areas of the hotel. It was obviously done to assure the hotel of having those special qualities that bring return guests. Ours is an age of specialization. Interior designers must be prepared to find their niche.

Jo Mielziner, the celebrated stage designer, was selected to handle the lighting and interior design for the grand ballroom, exhibit area, and meeting rooms. William Pahlmann was commissioned for the lobby areas and restaurants. Decor and furnishings of the guestrooms and suites were done by Joseph Huston. The consultant on lighting was Leslie Wheel. An extensive art program was planned for the hotel. Instead of reproductions, original paintings, etchings, lithographs, sculpture, and collages were commissioned for the guestrooms. Sculptor Ibram Lassaw began work in 1961 on a fused metal abstraction, fifteen feet long and ten feet high, to hang between the mezzanine and ballroom floors.

The New York Life Insurance Company put up the money for this newest of the grand hotels and two thoughts were probably uppermost in the minds of the investors: the promise of excellent convention facilities; and a hotel designed to function as economically as possible. At one time the magic ingredient for a new hotel was elegance. Today that ingredient is automation. Hotel men talk of giving greater service to offset the casual atmosphere of the motel, but a 2,000-room hotel can no longer cater personally to the guest. It can make him comfortable in a warm and cheerful bedroom and provide a sparkling bath; but ice cubes cannot be delivered to his room as they were when E. M. Statler started out in the business. It is impossible to man a switchboard for his every call on the telephone. Enough clerks to make the additions to his bill each night cannot be hired, nor can enough kitchen help to hand-squeeze his orange juice in the morning. Often it is difficult even to find someone willing to shine his shoes in the barbershop. The maid will still make up the room and the bellboy will still get the luggage to and from the lobby, but both will be equipped with transistor radio receivers so they can be given orders in any part of the hotel.

Nobody can guess at the limits of efficiency that can be reached with electronic controls and computers. Research into automation has been one of the major projects at Cornell University's School of Hotel Administration. The August 1961 issue of the school's quarterly magazine carried a provocative report on the potential of computers for handling everything from reservations to billing, from payroll preparation to liquor control.

The article, serious in content, wound on a humorous note:

> It is possible to envision a self service hotel in which the guest operates an electronic room rack for himself, registers by use of a credit card, prepares his breakfast in his room using a self service meal dispenser and a high speed cooker, and checks out of the hotel, again using his credit card, without ever having come in contact with any of the personnel of the hotel. While this has a strong science fiction flavor, before it is dismissed entirely it should be remembered that as recently as twenty years ago the area of science fiction included atomic energy, satellites and all of automation as we know it today.
>
> The editors pointed out that the example was not frivolous, that changes in technology and changes in society that have taken place in the recent past can be expected to continue in the future. It is the course of good business planning to attempt to foresee these new developments and to profit from them.

Older hotels may worry over the costs of modernization and the installation of labor-saving devices, but there is no choice for the new ones.

A word about a good night's sleep. Recently, my wife and I stayed overnight in a motor hotel. She watched television until 2:00 a.m., at 3:00 a.m. she got up and made instant coffee, and at 4:00 a.m. the guest down the way flushed his very noisy toilet; at 5:00 a.m. the night clerk, in error, turned on the red flashing message-waiting signal, and at 6:00 a.m. the room ice maker started its manufacturing cycle.

Richard B. Ziegler
Pick Hotels Corporation

There is no gainsaying a machine that takes only one minute to post the bills for one thousand guestrooms.

Bob Tisch agrees that a chrome-plated robot can never replace the friendliness of a neatly uniformed bellman, but his Americana in New York incorporates all possible automation throughout its fifty floors and 2,000 rooms. Completely automatic are sixteen elevators plus two 35-passenger lifts serving the convention areas on the second and third floors. The 300-car garage clocks the cars in electronically and washes them automatically.

Every guestroom has a bar-refrigerator which cuts out repeated room service except for meals. As in all new hotels, telephone service provides direct dialing, including long distance. All hotel service calls are set up for single-digit dialing and all telephones are equipped with message reminders.

In the kitchen, in addition to every imaginable food processing machine, a garbage disposal system grinds all forms of waste into a pulp, extracts the water and then blows it through a tube to a waiting truck outside.

At the front office is an electronic system that monitors control of room occupancy. A bank of red and green lights indicates the status of every room in the hotel.

The Americana has incorporated in its convention facilities one of Gotham's finest theatres with a four-level, hydraulically operated stage. An automatic coat-checking system insures few delays for convention delegates and banquet guests. Final touch, the electric shoe-shine machine will do everything but replace laces for half a dollar.

Hotel owners are prone to complain that designers are careless in matters of practicality. In talking with A. M. Sonnabend of Hotel Corporation of America during preparation for this book, he mentioned that he had seen advertisements by Sheraton that stressed the conveniences of bedside control of lighting and television in one of the chain's new hotels. Sonnabend said he was intrigued because, as he put it, "In so many of our newly decorated bedrooms, you either have to get out of bed or sit up to turn off the light."

I suggested that price has something to do with the amount of convenience provided to guests and reminded him that in the Room of Tomorrow I did for the 1958 hotel exposition, a bedside panel was incorporated which controlled lighting, television, clock-radio, cooling, and heat. Not only that, but it could change two slip-covered sofas into full size twin beds with the flick of a switch. "I think that too often we sacrifice convenience for beauty," he said.

The Room of Tomorrow has proved to be a stimulating program for American hotel men. In the portfolio of photographs at the end of this chapter, are those created by Tom Lee, Emily Malino, Marion Heuer, and Roy Beal. Each has contributed greatly to solving problems of efficiency in smaller spaces.

In a speech made to the 1961 convention of the California Hotel Association at Santa Barbara, architect Welton Becket predicted that in the year 2011 the hotel guest would get to his room and find his luggage already delivered by special elevator-conveyor. In the 1958 Room of Tomorrow, this very feature was incorporated. It could also be used for speedy room service, would provide more privacy for hotel guests and could dispatch soiled dishes and glasses quickly.

Becket also predicted that the hotel guest in the 21st century will arrive by a jetocopter and ride a moving corridor to a bank of computers in which he will insert a pre-punched reservation card. Then out will pop his key and room number. Current research studies indicate such a system will be possible long before the next century arrives.

Becket's dream hotel will also make extensive use of luminous panels that store sunlight during the day and feed it back at night at any desired intensity. Among other things to anticipate are: full-wall color television, electronic control of opaqueness in window and wall materials which will make solar screens and draperies unnecessary, and food service in the guestroom by means of computer punch cards.

But with all this promise of mechanical advance, Becket wisely reminds us that the emotional climate of a hotel must not be forgotten.

As psychologists develop definite theories of how to cater to our guests' emotional needs, we will design a hotel room that can be adjusted by the guest to his particular mood of the moment through changing color and light: If the guest is depressed, he can provide himself with gay colors. But if he wants a calming influence, he can adjust his room controls so that fabrics take on relaxing shades.

Becket left his audience with an admonition.

Most advances in hotel design and construction will be partially due to you. While we always do a tremendous amount of research for every new project we undertake, it is you, the client, whom we depend upon for direction based upon your operating experience. You must give us the same freedom to use our technology. The real advances in architectural design have been accomplished by an enlightened client who has faith in his architect.

The same holds true for interior design. Throughout these pages we have seen that the truly outstanding hotels and motels have been those in which a high degree of sophistication, talent, and experience has been contributed by client, architect, and designer.

There is no short cut that will eliminate any of the three.

ACKNOWLEDGMENTS

During the Chicago Market of 1960, Charles Whitney, over a late nightcap in the Ambassador's Buttery, suggested that I write a book on hotels and motor hotels. "That's fine, but how does one get started?" I asked, "You know I've had absolutely no experience." "Well, you've had experience in hotel design, so why don't you just put your thoughts down on paper and let me see them?"

During the next few months, on 'planes and during spare moments, I put together a skeleton projection of contents; this book is the final result. To publisher Charles Whitney, therefore, is my first indebtedness for encouraging me to summarize the unique history of hotel design (although he is in no way responsible for the shortcomings of the book). Some ideas and examples in this book will be familiar to readers of *Interiors*; I am most grateful to its eminently capable editor, Olga Gueft, and to her staff, who opened their files and sources and gave me much help. The text refers to many of the sources that I have used most extensively. If the reader wishes to pursue the subject further, there are a few books and periodicals which are enjoyable and useful and I have used with pleasure and profit the files of many of the magazines which are listed in the bibliography. *The American Hotel*, by Jefferson Williamson, is one source which I would particularly like to mention because it was extremely helpful to me; another is a special issue on hotels by Britain's *Architectural Review*; and a third from which I derived much amusement and pleasure on re-reading is Russell Lynes' *The Tastemakers*.

I wish to thank the librarian and staff members of the New York Public Library and of the New York Historical Society, and I am grateful to the many hotel leaders who were willing to take precious time off to talk into my tape recorder, answering questions about the problems of design and management. Thanks are also due to Bill Atkin, head of the book division of the Whitney Library, who, with editor Joan Adler, displayed a patience far beyond the call of good manners.

While I have unashamedly picked the brains of a good many architects and designers, I have not done so disrespectfully and I wish to acknowledge my indebtedness to them with the hope that I have done no injustice to their dedication to their work or ideas.

Last, but far from least, very special thanks go to Fred Sherman of the Miami Herald who miraculously made order out of the chaos of thoughts and words that I dictated to him.

BIBLIOGRAPHY

The following is by no means an exhaustive list of references but these are the literary sources which I myself have found most useful in studying hotel and motel design and the reader who is interested in pursuing the subject will find these a useful starting point.

BOOKS, PAMPHLETS, PAPERS

Ahrens Pub. Co., *A Pictorial Survey of the Hotel and Restaurant Markets*, New York

Allsopp, Bruce, *Decorations and Furniture*, Sir Isaac Pitman & Sons, Ltd, London, England, 1951

Architectural Record, *Building Types Study — Motels*, F. W. Dodge Corp., New York, April 1955

Carney, Clive, *Impact of Design*, Lawson Press Pty. Ltd., Sydney, Australia

Fickle, B. E., *Hotel Management and Related Subjects*, Cornell University Annual, Ithaca, N.Y.

Fry, Roger, *Transformations*, Doubleday, New York, 1956

Hoffman, Julius, Verlag, *Gaststatten*, Stuttgart, Germany, 1957

W. S. Hattrell and Partners, *Hotels, Restaurants, Bars*, Reinhold Publishing Corp., New York, 1962

Hotel Red Book, American Hotel Association, 221 West 57th Street, New York, N.Y.

Hotel World Review, *75 years of Hotel History*, (special anniversary number) Chicago, 1950

L'Architecture d'Aujourd 'hui, *Hotels-Cafes-Restaurants*, Boulogne, France, 1955

Lundy, Robert B., *Historic Hotels of the World, Past and Present*, Philadelphia, 1927

Lynes, Russell, *The Tastemakers*, Harper & Bros., Boston, 1949

American Institute of Interior Designers, *Manual of Professional Practice*, New York, 1955

Minnegerode, Meade, *The Fabulous Forties*, New York, 1924

F. W. Dodge Corp., *Motels, Hotels, Restaurants and Bars*, New York, 1953

Parker, William Stanley and Faneiril Adams, *The A.I.D. Standard Contract Forms and the Law*, Little Brown & Company, Boston, 1954

Pevsner, Nikolaus, *An Outline of European Architecture*, Penguin Book Ltd., Harmondsworth, Middlesex, England

Volume Feeding Management, *Operating Handbook*, New York, 1959

Williamson, Jefferson, *The American Hotel*, Alfred A. Knopf, New York, 1930

World Contemporary Architecture, Nuki Koganei-machi, Tokyo, Japan

MAGAZINES

American Innkeeper

Architectural Forum, Time, Inc., Time-Life Building, New York City, Monthly

Architectural Record, F. W. Dodge Corp., 19 East 40th Street, New York City, Monthly

Architectural Review, 9-13 Queen Anne's Gate, London, S.W.1, England, Monthly

Contract, 566 Seventh Avenue, New York City, Monthly

Cornell Hotel and Restaurant Administration Quarterly, School of Hotel and Restaurant Administration, Cornell University, Ithaca, New York

Dank Kunst Haand Vaenk, Palaegade 4 Mezz., Copenhagen, K, Denmark

Design, Council of Industrial Design, 28 Haymarket, London, S.W.1, England, Monthly

Domus, via Monte di Pieta 15, Milan, Italy, Monthly

Florida Architecture, 122 N. E. 39th Street, Miami, Annual

Hotel Bulletin, 200 Park Avenue, South, New York City, Monthly

Hotel Gazette, 33 Flatbush Avenue, Brooklyn, New York, Monthly

Hotel Monthly, 105 W. Adams, Chicago, Illinois, Monthly

Hotel-World Review, 230 Park Avenue, New York City, Bi-Weekly

Institutions, Domestic Engineering Co., 1801 Prairie Avenue, Chicago, Illinois, Monthly

Interior, P. O. Box 15009, Stockholm, Sweden, Monthly

Interior Design, 151 East 50th Street, New York City, Monthly

Interior Design, The National Trade Press Ltd., Drury House, Russell Street, London W.C. 2

Interiors, Whitney Publications, 18 East 50th Street, New York City, Monthly

International Lighting Review, P. O. Box 174, Amsterdam, Netherlands, Monthly

Moebel Interior Design, Danneckerstrasse 52, Stuttgart, Germany, Monthly

Progressive Architecture, Reinhold Publishing Corp., 430 Park Avenue, New York, Monthly

Southern Hotel Journal

INDEX